Richard Price

Additional observations on the nature and value of civil liberty, and the war with America

also, observations on schemes for raising money by public loans

Richard Price

Additional observations on the nature and value of civil liberty, and the war with America
also, observations on schemes for raising money by public loans

ISBN/EAN: 9783744738286

Printed in Europe, USA, Canada, Australia, Japan

Cover: Foto ©ninafisch / pixelio.de

More available books at **www.hansebooks.com**

ADDITIONAL OBSERVATIONS

On the NATURE and VALUE of

CIVIL LIBERTY,

AND THE

WAR WITH AMERICA:

ALSO

OBSERVATIONS on Schemes for raising Money by PUBLIC LOANS;

An Historical Deduction and Analysis of the NATIONAL DEBT;

And a brief Account of the DEBTS and RESOURCES of FRANCE.

Should the morals of the English be perverted by luxury;—should they lose their Colonies by restraining them, &c.—they will be enslaved; they will become insignificant and contemptible; and *Europe* will not be able to shew the world one nation in which she can pride herself.

ABBÉ RAYNAL.

By RICHARD PRICE, D.D. F.R.S.

THE SECOND EDITION.

LONDON:
Printed for T. CADELL, in the STRAND.
M.DCC.LXXVII.
[Price Two Shillings and Six-pence.]

Entered at STATIONER's-HALL, according to Act of Parliament.

TO

THE RIGHT HONOURABLE

THE LORD MAYOR,

THE ALDERMEN, AND THE COMMONS

OF THE

CITY OF LONDON,

THIS TRACT,

Containing ADDITIONS to thofe OBSERVATIONS
on CIVIL LIBERTY,

which they have honoured with their Approbation,

Is, with the greateſt Reſpect and Gratitude,

INSCRIBED,

BY

Their moſt obedient

and humble Servant,

RICHARD PRICE.

CONTENTS.

	Page
INTRODUCTION	vii

PART I.

SECT. I. *Of the* NATURE *of* Civil *Liberty, and the Essentials of a Free Government.* 1

SECT. II. *Of the* VALUE *of Liberty, and the* EXCELLENCE *of a Free Government.* — 15

CONCLUSION. 41

PART II.

SECT. I. *Supplemental Observations on the Surplus of the Revenue; the Quantity of Coin in the Kingdom; and Paper Credit.* — 53

SECT. II. *Of the State of the Nation; and the War with America.* — 69

SECT. III. *Of Schemes for raising Money by public Loans.* 89

PART III.

SECT. I. *Abstract of the* EXPORTS *from, and* IMPORTS *to* GREAT BRITAIN *from* 1697 *to* 1773, *with Remarks.* — 113

SECT. II. *Historical Deduction and Analysis of the Public Debts.* — 119

SECT. III. *Of the* DEBTS *and* RESOURCES *of* FRANCE. — 148

SECT. IV. *Remarks on the Earl of* STAIR'S *Account of the Public Income and Expenditure.* 156

Resolution of a Committee of the American *Congress in June* 1775. — 175

Published by the same Author,

And printed for T. CADELL, in the Strand.

I. OBSERVATIONS on REVERSIONARY PAYMENTS; on Schemes for providing Annuities for Widows, and Persons in Old Age; on the Method of calculating the Values of Assurances on Lives; and on the National Debt. To which are added, Four Essays on different Subjects in the Doctrine of Life-Annuities and Political Arithmetic. Also, an Appendix, containing a complete Set of Tables; particularly four New Tables, shewing the Probabilities of Life in LONDON, NORWICH, and NORTHAMPTON, and the Values of two joint Lives. The 3d Edition, with a Supplement, containing (besides several New Tables) additional Observations on the Probabilities of Human Life in different Situations; on the LONDON Societies for the Benefit of Widows and of Old Age; and on the present State of Population in this Kingdom. Price 6s.

II. A Review of the principal Questions and Difficulties in MORALS. Particularly, those relating to the Original of our Ideas of Virtue, its Nature, Foundation, Reference to the Deity, Obligation, Subject-matter, and Sanctions. The Second Edition corrected. Price 6s.

III. FOUR DISSERTATIONS.——I. On Providence.— II. On Prayer.—III. On the Reasons for expecting that virtuous Men shall meet after Death in a State of Happiness. —IV. On the Importance of Christianity, the Nature of Historical Evidence, and Miracles. The 4th Edition. Price 6s.

IV. An APPEAL to the PUBLIC, on the Subject of the NATIONAL DEBT. The 2d Edition; with an Appendix, containing Explanatory Observations and Tables; and an Account of the present State of Population in Norfolk. Price 2s.

V. OBSERVATIONS on the Nature of CIVIL LIBERTY, the Principles of GOVERNMENT, and the Justice and Policy of the WAR with AMERICA. To which is added, an Appendix, containing a State of the National Debt, an Estimate of the Money drawn from the Public by the Taxes, and an Account of the National Income and Expenditure since the last War. The 7th Edition. Price 2s.

INTRODUCTION.

BEFORE the reader enters on the following tract, I shall beg leave to detain him while I give a general account of the contents of it, and make a few introductory observations.

In the first part of the *Observations on Civil Liberty*, published last winter, I gave a brief account of the nature of Liberty in general, and of *Civil Liberty* in particular. That account appears to me, after carefully reconsidering it, to be just; nor do I think it in my power to improve it. In order, however, to be as explicit as possible on this subject, and to remove those misapprehensions of my sentiments into which some have fallen, I have thought proper to add the *supplemental* and *explanatory* observations, which will be found in the FIRST part of this pamphlet.——In writing with this view, I have been led to refer often to my former pamphlet, and to repeat some of the observations in it. But as this could not have been avoided, it will, I hope, be excused.

The remarks in the SECOND part, I offer to the public with all the deference due to the high station and abilities of the noble Lord, whose speech at opening the Budget in *April* last, has occasioned them.——These remarks, having been

A 4   promised

promised long ago, should have been published sooner. The reasons which have produced this delay are of little consequence to the public; and, therefore, need not be mentioned.

In the first section of this *second* part, it will, I think, appear, that I went upon as good grounds as the nature of the case admitted, when I stated the gold coin (a) of the kingdom at ABOUT TWELVE MILLIONS AND A HALF. It appears now, indeed, to be some millions more. But this is a discovery made by the call of last summer; which, I find, has brought in near double the sum that the best judges expected. Nothing, however, very encouraging can be inferred from hence. It only shews that a great deal of gold has been hoarded; and will, probably, be again hoarded. This is the natural consequence of public diffidence; and it is a circumstance which may, hereafter, greatly increase distress. Before the REVOLUTION, according to Dr. *Davenant*, near half the coin was hoarded; and the same, undoubtedly, will be done again, whenever the nation comes to be thoroughly alarmed.

In the next section of this part, I have made some further observations on the contest with *America*.———I cannot expect any other than a tragical and deplorable issue to this contest. But let events turn out as they will, I shall always

---

(a) See Observations on Civil Liberty, page 74.

reflect

reflect with satisfaction, that I have, though a private person of little consequence, bore my testimony, from deep-felt conviction, against a war which must shock the feelings and the reason of every considerate person; a war in which rivers of blood must be shed, not to repel the attacks of enemies, or to maintain the authority of government *within* the realm, but to maintain sovereignty and dominion in another world (*a*).—I wish the advocates for the measures against *America* would attend to the distinction now intimated.—The support of just government *within* the realm is always necessary, and therefore right. But to maintain, by fire and sword, dominion over the persons and the property of a people *out* of the realm, who have no share in its legislature, contradicts every principle of liberty and humanity.—Legitimate government, let it be remembered, as opposed to oppression and tyranny, consists " only in the dominion of " EQUAL LAWS made with COMMON CONSENT, or of " men over THEMSELVES ; and not in the dominion " of communities over communities, or of ANY " MEN OVER OTHER MEN."—This is the great truth I have endeavoured to explain and defend; and

(*a*) Of all the writers against this war, the learned Dr. TUCKER is the severest. For if, as he maintains, contrary to repeated declarations from the throne, a separation from the Colonies would be an advantage to us, the attempt to keep them, by invasion and bloodshed, deserves a harsher censure than words can convey.

happy

happy would the world be, were a due conviction of it impreſſed on every human heart.

The repreſentation I have given in this ſection and elſewhere, of the ſtate of this kingdom, is, without doubt, gloomy. But it is not the effect, as ſome have intimated, of either a natural diſpoſition to gloominefs, or of ſiniſter views. Few, who know me, will entertain ſuch a ſuſpicion. Valuing *moſt* what politicians and ſtateſmen generally value *leaſt*, I feel myſelf perfectly eaſy with reſpect to my intereſt as a citizen of this world; nor is there any change of ſituation that can make me happier, except a return to privacy and obſcurity. The opinion I have entertained of the preſent danger of the kingdom is, therefore, the effect of evidence which appears to me irreſiſtible. This evidence I have ſtated to the public; and every one may judge of it as he pleaſes. I am ſenſible of my own liableneſs to error. The meaſures which I condemn as the worſt that ever diſgraced and hazarded a great kingdom, others, whoſe integrity I cannot queſtion, approve; and that very ſituation of our affairs which I think alarming, others think proſperous. Time will determine which of theſe opinions is right. But ſuppoſing the latter to be ſo, no harm can ariſe from any repreſentations which have a tendency to put us on our guard.

I have beſtowed particular attention on the obſervations in the third ſection of this ſecond part;

and

and I think the subject of this section so important, that it is probable, I should not have resolved on the present publication, had it not been for the opportunity it gives me to lay the observations it contains before the public.——An intimation of them was given in the Introduction to the third edition of the Treatise on *Reversionary Payments*. The nation being now once more got into a course of borrowing; and our first step having been a return to a mode of borrowing, which had appeared to me absurd and detrimental, I was induced to resume the subject, and to examine it with more care. And the result of an examination of only a *part* of the public loans, will be found to be, " that a capital of more than " TWENTY MILLIONS has been a needless addition " to the public debt, for which no money, or any " sort of equivalent has been received; and which " might have been avoided, together with a great " expence of interest, by only forming differently " the schemes of the public loans."

The intention of the first section of the THIRD PART is to give, in as short a compass as possible, a view of the progress of our *foreign trade*, and its effect on the nation, from the beginning of this century; and, particularly, to point out an unfavourable change which seems to have taken place since 1764.

In the second section of this part, an explanation and analysis are given of all the different articles

articles of the national debt, which will probably inform every perſon of moſt that he can wiſh to know concerning them.—I have added a general account of the debts and reſources of FRANCE. This is a ſubject at preſent particularly intereſting to this country; and, having been informed of ſome important facts relating to it, I have thought proper to lay them before the public, with ſuch reflexions as have offered themſelves in mentioning them.

The laſt ſection contains ſuch of the calculations in the APPENDIX to the *Obſervations on Civil Liberty* as were neceſſary to be reprinted, in order to introduce the remarks I have added on ſome particulars in the ſtate of the *public income and expenditure*, publiſhed not long ago by the *Earl of Stair*. I have alſo meant to accommodate the purchaſers of the different editions of the *Obſervations on Civil Liberty*, who will be enabled, by this ſection, to poſſeſs themſelves of all the material alterations and improvements which were made in that pamphlet after its firſt publication.— The accounts, in the latter part of this tract, are ſo various and extenſive, that it is ſcarcely poſſible there ſhould not be ſome incorrectneſſes in them. But the pains I have taken, and the means of information which I have poſſeſſed have been ſuch, that I cannot ſuſpect that I have fallen into any miſtakes of conſequence. Should, however, any ſuch have eſcaped me, it will be kind in any person to point them out with candour; and to assist in making those accounts so correct and perfect, as that they may serve for a basis to all future accounts of the same kind.—The whole concludes with an account of a resolution drawn up in a Committee of the *American* Congress in 1775, disclaiming Independence, and offering an annual contribution to *Britain* for discharging its debts.

Such will be found to be the contents of the following work.——Throughout the whole of it, I have avoided entering into any controversy with the crowd of writers who have published remarks on my former pamphlet. I am, however, unwilling to overlook them entirely; and therefore, shall in this place, once for all, settle my accounts with them.

In the first place. Those friends (all unknown to me) who have published Vindications of me, whether in separate pamphlets, or in any of the periodical publications, will, I hope, accept my gratitude; and believe, that, though I have been silent, I have not been inattentive to their arguments, or insensible of their candour.

Secondly. Those writers of opposite sentiments, who have answered me without abuse or rancour, will also, I hope, accept my acknowledgments.— In this number I rank the writers of the pieces
enume-

enumerated below (a)——Thefe pieces contain, I believe, all of moſt importance which has been urged againſt me in the way of argument; and I leave every one who has read them, or ſhall read them, to decide for himſelf how far they have ſucceeded; only deſiring the juſtice may be done me, not to receive too eaſily any of the repreſentations made in them of my ſentiments. I have had, in this reſpect, ſome reaſon to complain of the faireſt of my adverſaries.

Thirdly. I muſt farther acknowledge myſelf indebted to thoſe writers, who, under the name of Anſwers, have publiſhed virulent invectives againſt me. It has been ſome gratification to me to obſerve, the alarm theſe writers have taken, and the folly they have diſcovered, by ſuffering themſelves to forget, that abuſe and ſcurrility always defeat their own ends, and hurt the cauſe they are employed to ſerve. I will not attempt to give any liſt of them. They are without number. But there is *one* who, being the ableſt, it is proper I ſhould mention. I mean, the author of the three Letters

---

(a) *Experience preferable to Theory*, printed for Payne.—— *Remarks on a pamphlet lately publiſhed, in a Letter from a Gentleman in the Country to a Member of Parliament*. Mr. Goodricke's Obſervations, &c. and Mr. Hey's; all printed for Mr. Cadell. ——Alſo Mr. *Weſley*'s and Mr. *Fletcher*'s Anſwers.——There may, perhaps, be ſome other Anſwers of the ſame kind; but they have not happened to fall into my hands.

to Dr. *Price*, published for Mr. *Payne*.——This writer is likewise the author of the *Letters on the Present State of Poland*; and of the *Remarks on the Acts of the thirteenth Parliament of Great Britain*; but he has been lately more known as a writer in the news-papers, under the signature of ATTILIUS; and also, as the supposed author of the *Answer to the American Declaration of Independence*.—— The following particulars will enable those, who may not yet know him sufficiently, to judge of his principles and temper.

Civil liberty, he insists, is nothing positive. It is, an *Absence*. The absence of *coercion*; or of *con*straint and *re*straint.—Not from civil governors, (they are OMNIPOTENT, and there can be no liberty (*a*) against them.)——But from such little despots and plunderers as common pick-pockets, thieves, house-breakers, &c.

Again. Having had occasion, in my *Observations on Civil Liberty*, page 42, to take some notice of him, I studied to mention him with respect. In return for this civility he has, in his three

(*a*) Their power is, however, acknowledged to be a TRUST; but not from the *people*. It must then be a trust from GOD; like the power of the proprietor of an estate over his tenants and cattle.—— Charming doctrine this for *Russia* and *Turkey!* And yet such is the doctrine, which this good Barrister, Mr. *Wesley*, Dr. *Cooper*, and others, are now propagating in this country. See *Three Letters*, page 66, &c. See likewise page 23 and 31, of the following tract.

letters

letters juſt mentioned, made me the object of an abuſe, which would have been inexcuſable had I offered him the groſſeſt affront.

Further. Such is the rage into which he has been thrown, that, imagining my notions of liberty and government have been drawn from the writings of the philoſophers of antient GREECE and ROME, he laments " that the *Goths* and " *Vandals*, ſparing their vaſes and urns, did not " deſtroy all their books of philoſophy and po- " litics." (*a*)—I am much miſtaken if he does not wiſh likewiſe, that all ſuch writings were de- ſtroyed as thoſe of *Sidney*, *Locke*, *Monteſquieu*, *Blackſtone*, &c.

I have only to add, that I am truly aſhamed of having, in this introduction, had occaſion to ſay ſo much about myſelf. But, I hope, candid al- lowances will be made for it, when it is conſidered how much, for ſome time, has been ſaid and writ about me. I now leave an open field to all who ſhall pleaſe to take any farther notice of me. Wiſhing them the ſame ſatisfaction that I have felt in *meaning* to promote peace and juſtice, and looking higher than this world of ſtrife and tumult—I withdraw from politics.

(*a*) *Three Letters*, p. 48.

PART

PART I.

SUPPLEMENTAL OBSERVATIONS

ON THE

Nature and Value of Civil Liberty and Free Government.

SECT. I.

Of the Nature of Civil Liberty, and the Essentials of a Free Government.

WITH respect to Liberty in general there are two questions to be considered: First, What it is?—And Secondly, How far it is of value?

There is no difficulty in answering the first of these questions.—To be FREE, is " to be able to " act or to forbear acting, as we think best;" or " to be masters of our own resolutions and con- " duct."——It may be pretended, that it is not desirable to be thus free; but, without doubt, this it is to be *free*; and this is what all mean when

when they say of themselves or others that they are *free*.

I have observed, that all the different kinds of Liberty run up into the general idea of self-government (*a*).——The Liberty of men as *agents* is that power of self-determination which all agents, as such, possess.—Their Liberty as *moral* agents is their power of self-government in their *moral* conduct.—Their Liberty as *religious* agents is their power of self-government in *religion*.——And their Liberty, as members of communities associated for the purposes of civil government, is their power of self-government in all their civil concerns. It is Liberty, in the last of these views of it, that is the subject of my present enquiry; and it may, in other words, be defined to be " the power of a state to govern itself by its own " will."——In order, therefore, to determine whether a state is free, no more is necessary than to determine whether there is any will, different from its own, to which it is subject.

When we speak of a state, we mean the *whole* state, and not any *part* of it; and the will of the state, therefore, is the will of the whole.—— There are two ways in which this will may be expressed. First, by the suffrages of all the members given in person. Or secondly, by the suf-

---
(*a*) See Observations on Civil Liberty, Part I. sect. 1.

frages

frages of a body of Reprefentatives, in appointing whom all the members have voices.——A ftate governed by its own will in the firft of thefe ways enjoys the moft complete and perfect Liberty; but fuch a government being impracticable, except in very fmall ftates, it is neceffary that civil communities in general fhould fatisfy themfelves with that degree of Liberty which can be obtained in the laft of thefe ways; and Liberty fo obtained may be fufficiently ample, and at the fame time is capable of being extended to the largeft ftates (*a*).

But here, before I proceed, I muft defire, that an obfervation may be attended to, which appears to me of confiderable confequence.——A diftinction fhould be made between the *Liberty* of a ftate, and its not fuffering oppreffion; or between a free government, and a government under which freedom is enjoyed. Under the moft defpotic government liberty may happen to be enjoyed. But being derived from a will over which the ftate has no controul, and not from its own will; or from an accidental mildnefs in the *adminiftration*, and not from a *conftitution* of government; it is nothing but an indulgence of a precarious nature, and of little importance.——Individuals in pri-

---

(*a*) See Obfervations, Part I. fect. 2.

vate life, while held under the power of masters, cannot be denominated free, however equitably and kindly they may be treated. This is strictly true of *communities* as well as of *individuals*.—— Civil Liberty (it should be remembered) must be enjoyed as a right derived from the Author of nature only, or it cannot be the blessing which merits this name. If there is any human power which is considered as *giving* it, on which it depends, and which can invade or recall it at pleasure, it changes its nature, and becomes a species of slavery.

But to return——The force superseding selfgovernment in a state, or the power destroying its Liberty, is of two kinds. It may be either a power *without* itself, or a power *within* itself. The former constitutes what may be properly called *external*, and the latter *internal* slavery.— Were there any distant state which had acquired a sovereignty over this country, and exercised the power of making its laws and disposing its property, we should be in the first kind of slavery; and, if not totally depraved by a habit of subjection to such a power, we should think ourselves in a miserable condition; and an advocate for such a power would be considered as insulting us, who should attempt to reconcile us to it by telling us, that we were *one* community with that distant

state,

state, though destitute of a single voice in its legislature; and, on this ground, should maintain, that all resistance to it was no less criminal than any resistance *within* a state to the authority of that state.—In short, every state, not incorporated with another by an equal representation, and yet subject to its dominion, is enslaved in this sense.— Such was the slavery of the provinces subject to antient *Rome*; and such is the slavery of every community, as far as any other community is master of it; or as far as, in respect of taxation and internal legislation, it is not independent of every other community. Nor does it make any difference to such a community, that it enjoys within itself a free constitution of government, if that constitution is itself liable to be altered, suspended or over-ruled at the discretion of the state which possesses the sovereignty over it.

But the slavery most prevalent in the world has been internal slavery.———In order better to explain this, it is proper to observe, that all civil government being either the government of a *whole* by *itself*, or of a *whole* by a *power extraneous* to it, or of a *whole* by a *part*; the first *alone* is LIBERTY, and the two last are TYRANNY, producing the two sorts of slavery which I have mentioned. Internal slavery, therefore, takes place wherever a whole community is governed by a *part*; and this, perhaps, is the most concise and

comprehenfive account that can be given of it.—
The part that governs may be either a *fingle* man,
as in *abfolute Monarchies*; or, a body of grandees,
as in *Ariftocracies*. In both thefe cafes the
powers of government are commonly held for
life without delegation, and defcend from father
to fon; and the people governed are in the fame
fituation with cattle upon an eftate, which defcends
by inheritance from one owner to another.——
But farther. A community may be governed by
a body of delegates, and yet be enflaved.——
Though government by reprefentation alone is
free, unlefs when carried on by the perfonal fuf-
frages of all the members of a ftate, yet *all* fuch
government is by no means free. In order to
render it fo, the following requifites are neceffary.

Firft, The reprefentation muft be *complete*. No
ftate, a *part* of which only is reprefented in the
Legiflature that governs it, is *felf*-governed.
Had *Scotland* no reprefentatives in the Parliament
of *Britain*, it would not be free; nor would it be
proper to call *Britain* free, though *England*, its
other part, were adequately reprefented. The
like is true, in general, of every country fubject to
a Legiflature in which *fome* of its parts, or fome
claffes of men in it, are reprefented, and others
not.

Secondly, The reprefentatives of a free ftate
muft be *freely* chofen. If this is not the cafe, they
are

are not at all representatives; and government by them degenerates into government by a junto of men in the community, who happen to have power or wealth enough to command or purchase their offices.

Thirdly, After being *freely* chosen, they must be themselves *free*. If there is any higher will which directs their resolutions, and on which they are dependent, they become the instruments of that will; and it is that will alone that in reality governs the state.

Fourthly, They must be chosen for short terms; and, in all their acts, be accountable to their constituents. Without this a people will have no controul over their representatives; and, in chusing them, they will give up entirely their Liberty; and only enjoy the poor privilege of naming, at certain intervals, a set of men whom they are to *serve*, and who are to dispose, at their discretion, of their property and lives.

The causes of internal slavery now mentioned prevail, some of them more and others less, in different communities. With respect, in particular, to a government by representation; it is evident, that it deviates more or less from Liberty, in proportion as the representation is more or less imperfect. And, if imperfect in every one of the instances I have recited; that is, if inadequate and partial; subject to no controul from the people;

people; corruptly chosen for long terms; and, after being chosen, venal and dependent;—in these circumstances, a representation becomes an imposition and a nusance; and government by it is as inconsistent with true Liberty as the most arbitrary and despotic government.

I have been so much misunderstood (*a*) on this subject, that it is necessary I should particularly observe here, that my intention in this account has been merely to shew what is requisite to constitute a state or a government free, and not at all to define the best form of government. These are two very different points. The first is attended with few difficulties. A free state is a state self-governed in the manner I have described. But it may be free, and yet not enjoy the best constitution of government. Liberty, though the most essential requisite in government, is not the only one. Wisdom, union, dispatch, secresy, and vigour are likewise requisite; and that is the best form of government which best unites all these qualities; or which, to an equal and perfect Liberty, adds the greatest

(*a*) The greatest part of Mr. *Goodricke*'s remarks are founded on this misunderstanding. He is so candid that I know he did not mean to misrepresent me; and yet I cannot help thinking it hard, after repeated declarations of my preference of such a constitution as our own, to be considered as an advocate for a pure Democracy. See *Observations on Dr. Price's Theory and Principles of Civil Liberty and Government*, by Mr. GOODRICKE.

wisdom

wisdom in deliberating and resolving, and the greatest union, force and expedition in executing *(a)*.

In short, my whole meaning is, that the will of the Community alone ought to govern; but that there are different methods of obtaining and executing this will; of which those are the best which collect into it most of the knowledge and experience of the community, and at the same time carry it into execution with most dispatch and vigour.

It has been the employment of the wisest men in all ages to contrive plans for this purpose; and the happiness of society depends so much on civil government, that it is not possible the human understanding should be better employed.

I have said in the Observations on Civil Liberty, that " in a free state every man is his own le-" gislator."—I have been happy in since finding the *(b)* same assertion in *Montesquieu*, and also in

---

(a) One of the best plans of this kind has been with much ability, described by Mr. De Lolme, in his account of the Constitution of England.

(b) " As in a free state, every man who is supposed a free " agent, ought to be his own governor; so the legislative " power should reside in the whole body of the people." *Spirit of Laws*, Book XI. chap. vi. See likewise Justice Blackstone's Commentaries on the Laws of England, page 158. 1st Vol. oct. edition.——*Demosthenes* speaking in his first Philippic, sect. 3d. of certain free states, calls them *their own legislators*, αυτονομουμενα και ελευθερα.

Mr.

Mr. Justice *Blackstone*'s Commentaries. It expresses the fundamental principle of our constitutution; and the meaning of it is plainly, that every independent agent in a free state ought to have a share in the government of it, either by himself *personally*, or by a body of representatives, in chusing whom he has a free vote, and therefore all the concern and weight which are possible, and consistent with the equal rights of every other member of the state.——But though the meaning of this assertion is so obvious, and the truth of it undeniable, it has been much exclaimed against, and occasioned no small part of the opposition which has been made to the principles advanced in the *Observations on Civil Liberty*.——One even of the most candid, as well as the ablest of my opponents, (whose difference of opinion from me I sincerely lament) has intimated, that it implies, that, in a free state, (*a*) *thieves and pick-pockets have a right to make laws for themselves*.——The public will not, I hope, wonder that I chuse to take little notice of such objections.

It has been said, that the liberty for which I have pleaded, is " a right or power in every one

(*a*) See *Remarks*, printed for Mr. Cadell, *on a pamphlet published by Dr. Price. In a letter from a gentleman in the country to a member of parliament*, page 10.

" to

"to act as he likes without any restraint."―― However unfairly this representation has been given of my account of liberty, I am ready to adopt it, provided it is understood with a few limitations.――Moral Liberty, in particular, cannot be better defined than by calling it " a " power in every one to do as he likes." My opponents in general seem to be greatly puzzled with this; and I am afraid it will signify little to attempt explaining it to them by saying, that every man's will, if perfectly free from restraint, would carry him invariably to rectitude and virtue; and that no one who acts wickedly acts as he *likes*, but is conscious of a tyranny within him overpowering his judgment, and carrying him into a conduct, for which he condemns and hates himself. *The things that he would he does not*; (a) *and the things that he would not, those he does.* He is, therefore, a slave in the properest sense.

Religious Liberty, likewise, is a power of acting as we *like* in religion; or of professing and practising that mode of religious worship which we think most acceptable to the Deity.――But here the limitation to which I have referred must be attended to. All have the same unalienable right to this Liberty; and consequently, no one has a right to such a use of it as shall take it from others.

(a) Rom. vii.

Within this limit, or as far as he does not encroach on the equal liberty of others, every one has a right to do as he pleases in religion.—— That the right to religious Liberty goes as far as this every one muſt allow, who is not a friend to perſecution; and that it cannot go farther, is ſelf-evident; for if it did, there would be a contradiction in the natures of things; and it would be true, that every one had a right to enjoy what every one had a right to deſtroy.——If, therefore, the religious faith of any perſon leads him to hurt another becauſe he profeſſes a different faith; or if it carries him, in any inſtances, to intolerance, Liberty itſelf requires he ſhould be reſtrained, and that, in ſuch inſtances, he ſhould loſe his liberty.

All this is equally applicable to the Liberty of man in his *civil* capacity; and it is a maxim true univerſally, " that as far as any one does not " moleſt *others*, others ought not to moleſt *him*." ——All have a right to the free and undiſturbed poſſeſſion of their good names, properties and lives; and it is the right all have to this that gives the right to eſtabliſh civil government, which is or ought to be nothing but an inſtitution (by laws and proviſions made with *common* conſent) for guarding this right againſt invaſion; for giving to every one, in *temporals* and *ſpirituals*, the power of commanding his own conduct; or, of

acting

acting as he pleases, and going where he will, provided he does not run foul of others.——Juſt government, therefore, does not *infringe* liberty, but *eſtabliſh* it.——It does not *take away* the rights of mankind, but *protect* and *confirm* them.—— I will add, that it does not even create any new ſubordinations of particular men to one another, but only gives ſecurity in thoſe ſeveral ſtations, whether of authority and pre-eminence, or of ſub-ordination and dependence, which nature has eſtabliſhed, and which muſt have ariſen among mankind whether civil government had been inſtituted or not. But this goes beyond my purpoſe in this place, and more will be ſaid of it preſently.

To ſum up the whole—Our ideas of Civil Liberty will be rendered more diſtinct by conſidering it under the three following views:—The Liberty of the *citizen*—The liberty of the *government*—And the liberty of the *community*.——A *citizen* is free when the power of commanding his own conduct and the quiet poſſeſſion of his life, perſon, property and good name are *ſecured* to him by being his own legiſlator in the ſenſe explained in page 10 (*a*).——A *government* is free when conſtituted

---

(*a*) Dr. Priestly, in his Eſſay on the *firſt principles of Government*, makes a diſtinction between *civil* Liberty and *political* Liberty; the former of which he defines to be " the " power

constituted in such a manner as to give this *security*.——And the freedom of a community or nation is the same among nations, that the freedom of a citizen is among his fellow-citizens.——It is not, therefore, as observed in page 3, the mere possession of Liberty that denominates a citizen or a community free; but that *security* for the possession of it which arises from such a free government as I have described; and which takes place, when there exists no power that can take it away.——It is in the same sense that the mere performance of virtuous actions is not what denominates an agent virtuous; but the temper and habits from whence they spring; or that *inward constitution*, and right balance of the affections, which *secure* the practice of virtue, produce stability of conduct, and constitute a *character*.

I cannot imagine how it can be disputed whether this is a just account of the nature of Liberty. It has been already given more briefly in the Observations on Civil Liberty; and it is with reluctance I have repeated so much of what

" power which the members of a state ought to enjoy over
" their actions;" and the latter, " their power of arriving at
" public offices, or, at least, of having votes in the nomina-
" tion of those who fill them."—This distinction forms a very proper subdivision of *the liberty of the citizen* here mentioned; and it may be accommodated to all I have said on this subject, by only giving some less general name to that which Dr. Priestly calls *civil* Liberty.

has

has been there said. But the wrong apprehensions which have been entertained of my sentiments have rendered this necessary. And, for the same reason, I am obliged to go on to the subject of the next section.

SECT. II.

Of the VALUE *of Liberty, and the* EXCELLENCE *of a Free Government.*

HAVING shewn in the preceding section "what Liberty is;" the next question to be considered is, "how far it is valuable."

Nothing need be said to shew the value of the three kinds of liberty which I have distinguished under the names of *Physical, Moral,* and *Religious* Liberty. They are, without doubt, the foundation of all the happiness and dignity of men, as reasonable and moral agents, and the subjects of the Deity.—It is, in like manner, true of *Civil* Liberty, that it is the foundation of the whole happiness and dignity of men as members of civil society, and the subjects of civil government.

First. It is Civil Liberty, or such free government as I have described, that alone can give just security against oppression. One government is better than another in proportion as it gives more of this security. It is, on this account, that the supreme government of the Deity is perfect.

There

There is not a poffibility of being oppreffed or aggrieved by it. Subjection to it is the fame with complete freedom.

Were there any men on whofe fuperior wifdom and goodnefs we might abfolutely depend, they could not poffefs too much power; and the love of liberty itfelf would engage us to fly to them, and to put ourfelves under their direction. But fuch are the principles that govern human nature; fuch the weaknefs and folly of men; fuch their love of domination, felfifhnefs, and depravity; that none of them can be raifed to an elevation above others without the utmoft danger. The conftant experience of the world has verified this; and proved, that nothing intoxicates the human mind fo much as power, and that men, when they have got poffeffion of it, have feldom failed to employ it in grinding their fellow-men, and gratifying the vileft paffions.—In the eftablifhment, therefore, of civil government, it would be prepofterous to rely on the difcretion of any men. If a people would obtain fecurity againft oppreffion, they muft feek it in *themfelves*, and never part with the powers of government out *of their own* hands. It is there only they can be fafe.— A people will never opprefs themfelves, or invade their own rights. But if they truft the arbitrary will of any body or fucceffion of men, they truft

ENEMIES,

ENEMIES, and it may be depended on that the worst evils will follow.

It follows from hence, that a free government is the only government which is consistent with the ends of government.——Men combine into communities and institute government to obtain the peaceable enjoyment of their rights, and to defend themselves against injustice and violence: And when they endeavour to secure these ends by such a free government as I have described, improved by such arrangements as may have a tendency to preserve it from confusion, and to concentrate in it as much as possible of the wisdom and force of the community; In this case, it is a most rational and important institution.——But when the contrary is done; and the benefits of government are sought by establishing a government of *men*, and not of *laws* made with common consent; it becomes a most absurd institution.— It is seeking a remedy for oppression in *one* quarter, by establishing it in *another*; and avoiding the outrages of *little* plunderers, by constituting a set of *great* plunderers.——It is, in short, the folly of *giving up* liberty in order to *maintain* Liberty; and, in the very act of endeavouring to secure the most valuable rights, to arm a body of enemies with power to destroy them.

I can eafily believe, that mankind, in the firft and rude ftate of fociety, might act thus irrationally. Abfolute governments, being the fimpleft forms of government, might be the firft that were eftablifhed. A people having experienced the happy effects of the wifdom or the valour of particular men, might be led to truft them with unlimited power as their rulers and legiflators. But they would foon find reafon to repent: And the time, I hope, may come, when mankind in general, taught by long and dear experience, and *weary* of the abufes of power under *flavifh* governments, will learn to deteft them, and never to give up that SELF-GOVERNMENT, which, whether we confider men in their private or collective capacities, is the firft of all the bleffings they can poffefs.

Again. Free governments are the only governments which give fcope to the exertion of the powers of men, and are favourable to their improvement.——The members of free ftates, knowing their rights to be fecure, and that they fhall enjoy without moleftation the fruits of every acquifition they can make, are encouraged and incited to induftry. Being at liberty to pufh their refearches as far as they can into all fubjects, and to guide themfelves by their own judgments in all their religious and civil concerns, while they

allow

allow others to do the same; error and superstition must lose ground. Conscious of being their own governors, bound to obey no laws except such as they have given their consent to, and subject to no controul from the arbitrary will of any of their fellow-citizens; they possess an elevation and force of mind which must make them great and happy.——How different is the situation of the vassals of despotic power?——Like cattle inured to the yoke, they are driven on in one track, afraid of speaking or even thinking on the most interesting points; looking up continually to a poor creature who is their master; their powers fettered; and some of the noblest springs of action in human nature rendered useless within them. There is nothing indeed more humiliating than that debasement of mankind which takes place in such situations.

It has been observed of free governments, that they are often torn by violent contests, which render them dreadful scenes of distress and anarchy. But it ought to be considered, that this has not been owing to the *nature* of such governments; but to their having been ill-modelled, and wanted those arrangements and supplemental checks which are necessary to constitute a wise form of government.——There is no reason to doubt, but that free governments may be so contrived, as to exclude the greatest part of the struggles and tumults which have arisen in free states; and, as far as they cannot be excluded, they will do more good than harm. They will occasion the display of powers, and produce exertions which can never be seen in the *still* scenes of life. They are the active efforts of health and vigour; and always tend to preserve and purify. Whereas, on the contrary, the *quiet* which prevails under slavish governments, and which may seem to be a recommendation of them, proceeds from an ignominious tameness, and stagnation of the human faculties. It is the same with the *stillness* of midnight, or the *silence* and torpor of death.

Further. Free governments are the only governments which are consistent with the natural equality of mankind. This is a principle which, in my opinion, has been assumed, with the greatest reason, by some of the best writers on government. But the meaning of it is not, that all the subordinations in human life owe their existence to the institution of civil government. The superiorities and distinctions arising from the relation of parents to their children; from the differences in the personal qualities and abilities of men; and from servitudes founded on voluntary compacts, must have existed in a state of nature, and would now take place were all men so virtuous as to leave no occasion for civil government.——The maxim, therefore,

therefore, " that all men are naturally equal," refers to their state when grown up to maturity, and become independent agents, capable of acquiring property, and of directing their own conduct. And the sense of it is, that no one of them is constituted by the author of nature the vassal or subject of another, or has any right to give law to him, or, without his consent, to take away any part of his property, or to abridge him of his liberty.——In a state of nature, one man may have received benefits from another; and this would lay the person obliged under an obligation of gratitude, but it would not make his *benefactor* his *master*; or give him a right to judge for him what grateful returns he ought to make, and to extort these from him.——In a state of nature, also, one man may possess more strength, or more knowledge, or more property than another; and this would give him weight and influence; but it would not give him any degree of authority. There would not be one human being who would be bound to *obey* him.——A person likewise, in a state of nature, might let out his labour, or give up to another, on certain stipulated terms, the direction of his conduct; and this would so far bring him into the station of a *servant*; but being done by himself, and on such terms only as he chuses to consent to, it is an *instance* of his liberty;

and he will always have it in his power to quit the fervice he has chofen, or to enter into another.

This equality or independence of men is one of their effential rights. (*a*) It is the fame with that equality or independence which now actually takes place among the different ftates or kingdoms of the world with refpect to one another. Mankind came with this right from the hands of their Maker.——But all governments, which are not free, are totally inconfiftent with it. They imply, that there are fome of mankind who are born with an inherent right of dominion; and that the reft are born under an obligation to fubjection; and that civil government, inftead of being founded on any compact, is nothing but the exercife of this right. Some fuch fentiments feem to be now reviving in this country, and even to be growing fafhionable. Moft of the writers againft the *Obfervations on Civil Liberty* argue on the fuppofition of a right in the *few* to govern the *many* (*b*), independently

---

(*a*) See on this Subject an excellent Sermon entitled, *The Principles of the* REVOLUTION *vindicated*. By Dr. Watfon, Regius Profeffor of Divinity, at Cambridge.

(*b*) Some who maintain this doctrine concerning government, overthrow their own fyftem by acknowledging the right of refiftance in certain cafes. For, if there is fuch a right, the people muft be judges *when* it ought to be exercifed; a right to refift only when civil governors *think* there is reafon, being a grofs abfurdity and nullity.——The right of refiftance,

pendently, of their own choice. Some of these writers have gone so far as to assert, in plain language, that civil governors derive their power immediately from the Deity; and are *his* agents or representatives, accountable to him only. And one courtly writer, in particular, has honoured them with the appellation of OUR POLITICAL GODS. ——Probably, this is the idea of civil governors entertained by the author of the *Remarks on the Acts of the Thirteenth Parliament of Great Britain*: for it is not easy to imagine on what other ground he can assert, that *property* and *civil rights* are derived from civil governors, and their *gifts* to mankind (*a*).

sistance, therefore, cannot mean less than a right in the people, whenever they think it necessary, to change their governors, and to limit their power. And from the moment this is done, government becomes the work of the people, and governors become their trustees or agents.

(*a*) It has been commonly reckoned, that it is the end of civil government and civil laws to protect the *property* and *rights* of men; but, according to this writer, civil government and civil laws create *property* and *rights*. It follows therefore, that, antecedently to civil laws, men could have no *property* or *rights*; and that civil governors, being the makers of civil laws, it is a contradiction to suppose, that mankind can have any property or rights which are valid against the claims of their governors. See Three Letters to Dr. *Price*, p. 21, &c. And Remarks on the principal Acts of the 13th Parliament of Great-Britain, p. 58, &c. and p. 191.

If thefe fentiments are juft, civil governors are indeed an awful order of beings; and it becomes us to enquire with anxiety who they are, and how we may diftinguifh them from the reft of mankind.——Shall we take for fuch all, whether *men* or *women*, whom we find in actual poffeffion of civil power, whatever may be their characters; or however they may have acquired their power?—— This is too extravagant to be afferted. It would legalize the *American* Congrefs.——There muft then be fome *pretenders* among civil governors; and it is neceffary we fhould know how to difcover them. It is incredible, that the Deity fhould not have made this eafy to us, by fome particular marks and diftinctions, which point out to our notice his *real* vicegerents; juft as he has pointed out man, by his figure and fuperior powers, to be the governor of the lower creatures.——In particular; thefe perfons muft be poffeffed of wifdom and goodnefs fuperior to thofe of the reft of mankind (*a*); for, without this, a grant of the powers they are fuppofed to poffefs would be nothing but a grant of power to injure and opprefs, without remedy and without bounds. But this is a teft by which they cannot be tryed. It would leave but few of them in poffeffion of the places they

---

(*a*) This has been done in a lower inftance. Parents have been furnifhed with a particular affection for their children, in order to prevent any abufe of their power over them.

hold

hold and the rights they claim. It is not in the high ranks of life, or among the great and mighty, that we are to feek wifdom and goodnefs. Thefe love the fhade, and fly from obfervation. They are to be found chiefly in the middle ranks of life, and among the contemplative and philofophical, who decline public employments, and look down with pity on the fcramble for power among mankind, and the reftleffnefs and mifery of ambition.——It is proper to add, that it has never been hitherto underftood that any fuperiority in intellectual and moral qualifications lays the foundation of a claim to *dominion*.

It is not then, by their fuperior endowments, that the Deity intended to point out to us the *few* whom he has deftined to command the *many*. —But in what other manner could they be diftinguifhed?——Muft we embrace Sir *Robert Filmer*'s *Patriarchal* fcheme? One would have thought, that Mr. *Locke* has faid more than enough to expofe this ftupid fcheme. One of my opponents, however, has adopted it; and the neceffary inference from it is that, as there is but now one lineal defcendent from Adam's eldeft fon, there can be but one rightful monarch of the world.— But I will not abufe my reader's patience by faying more on this fubject. I am forry that in this country there fhould be any occafion for taking notice of principles fo abfurd, and at the

fame

same time so pernicious (a). I say, PERNICIOUS; for they imply, that King *James* the Second was deposed at the Revolution unlawfully and impiously; that the present King is an usurper; and that the present government, being derived from rebellion and treason, has no right to our allegiance.

Without all doubt, it is the choice of the people that makes civil governors.—The people are the spring of all civil power, and they have a right to modify it as they please.

(a) "In ages of darkness, and too often also in those of
" greater knowledge, by the perfidious arts of designing
" princes, and by the base servility of too many ecclesiastics,
" who managed the superstition of the populace, by the vio-
" lent restraints put upon divulging any juster sentiments
" about the rights of mankind, the natural notions of polity
" were erased out of the minds of men; and they were filled
" with some confused imaginations of something adorable in
" monarchs, some representation of the Divinity; and that
" even in the worst of them; and of some certain Divine
" claims in certain families.——No wonder this! that mil-
" lions thus look upon themselves as a piece of property to
" one of their fellows as silly and worthless as the meanest
" of them; when the like arts of superstition have made mil-
" lions, nay the very artificers themselves, fall down before
" the block or stone they had set up; or adore monkies, cats,
" and crocodiles, as the sovereign disposers of their fortunes."
See Dr. HUTCHESON's System of Moral Philosophy. Vol. ii. p. 280.

Mankind

Mankind being naturally equal according to the foregoing explanation, civil government, *in its genuine intention*, is an inftitution for maintaining that equality, by defending it againft the encroachments of violence and tyranny. All the fubordinations and diftinctions in fociety previous to its eftablifhment, it leaves as it found them, only confirming and protecting them. It makes no man *mafter* of another. It elevates no perfon above his fellow citizens. On the contrary, it levels all by fixing all in a ftate of fubjection to one common authority.——The authority of the laws.—The will of the community.——TAXES are *given*; not *impofed*. LAWS are regulations of common choice; not injunctions of fuperior power.——The authority of magiftrates is the authority of the State; and their falaries are wages paid by the State for executing its will and doing its bufinefs. *They* do not govern the *State*. It is the *State* governs *them*; and had they juft ideas of their own ftations, they would confider themfelves as no lefs properly *fervants* of the Public, than the labourers who work upon its roads, or the foldiers who fight its battles.—— A KING, in particular, is only the firft executive officer; the creature of the law; and as much accountable and fubject to the law as the meaneft peafant (*a*). And were Kings properly attentive

---

(*a*) " Let not, therefore, thefe *pretended mafters* of the
" people be allowed even to do good againft the general
" confent.

to their duty, and as anxious as they should be about performing it, they could not eafily avoid finking under the weight of their charge.

The account now given is, I am fully perfuaded, in every particular, a true account of what civil government *ought* to be; and it teaches us plainly the great importance and excellence of FREE Government.——It is this only that anfwers the defcription I have given of government; that fecures againft oppreffion; that gives room for that elevation of fpirit and that exertion of the human powers which is neceffary to human improvement; or that is confiftent with the ends of government, with the rights of mankind, and their natural equality and independence. *Free* Government, therefore, only, is *juft* and *legitimate* government.

It follows farther from the preceding account, that no people can lawfully furrender or cede their Liberty. This muft appear to any one

---

" confent.——Let it be confidered, that the condition of
" rulers is exactly the fame as that of the Cacique, who being
" afked whether he had any flaves, anfwered; *Slaves? I*
" *know but one flave in all my diftrict, and that is myfelf.*"
See the Philofophical and Political Hiftory of the Settlements and Trade of the *Europeans* in the EAST AND WEST INDIES. Tranflated from the French of the Abbé *Raynal*, by Mr. *Juftamond*. Vol. v. page 414.

who

who will confider, that when a people make such a ceffion, and the extenfive powers of government are trufted to the difcretion of any man or body of men, they part with the powers of life and death, and give themfelves up a prey to oppreffion; that they make themfelves the inftruments of any injuftice in which their rulers may chufe to employ them, by arming them againft neighbouring ftates; and alfo, that they do this not only for *themfelves*, but for their *pofterity*.——I will add, that if fuch a ceffion has been made; or if through any caufes, a people have loft their Liberty, they muft have a right to emancipate themfelves as foon as they can (*a*). In attempting this, indeed, they ought to confider the fufferings which may attend the ftruggle, and the evils which may arife from a defeat. But at the fame time, it will be proper to confider, that the fufferings attending fuch a ftruggle muft be temporary, whereas the evils to be avoided are permanent; and that Liberty is a bleffing fo ineftimable, " that whenever there appears any pro-
" bability of recovering it, a people fhould be
" willing to run many hazards, and even not to

(*a*) See Obf. p. 25. " The rights of mankind are fo facred " that no prefcription of tyranny or arbitrary power can have " authority enough to abolifh them." Mr. *Hume*'s Effays, vol. iii. Effay on the Coalition of Parties.

" repine.

" repine at the greateſt expence of blood or trea-
" ſure." (a)

I am very ſenſible, that civil government, as it actually exiſts in the world, by no means anſwers to the account I have given of it.——Inſtead of being an inſtitution for guarding the weak againſt the ſtrong, we find it an inſtitution which makes the ſtrong yet ſtronger, and gives them a ſyſtematical power of oppreſſing. Inſtead of promoting virtue and reſtraining vice, encouraging free enquiry, eſtabliſhing Liberty, and protecting alike all peaceable perſons in the enjoyment of their civil and religious rights; we ſee a ſavage deſpotiſm, under its name, laying waſte the earth, unreaſonably elevating ſome and depreſſing others, diſcouraging improvement, and trampling upon every human right. That force of ſtates, which ought to be applied only to their own defence, we ſee continually applied to the purpoſe of attack, and uſed to extend dominion by conquering neighbouring communities.——Civil governors conſider not themſelves as *ſervants* but as *maſters*. Their ſtations they think they hold in their own right. The people they reckon their property;

(a) " Mankind have been generally a great deal too tract-
" able; and hence ſo many wretched forms of power have
" always enſlaved nine tenths of the nations of the world,
" where they have the fulleſt right to make all efforts for a
" change." Dr. *Hutcheſon's* Moral Philoſophy. Vol. ii. p. 280.

and their poffeffions, a common *stock* from which they have a right to take what (*a*) they will, and of which no more belongs to any individual than they are pleafed to *leave* him.

What a miferable perverfion is this of a moft important inftitution? What a grievance is government fo degenerated?——But this perverfion furnifhes no juft argument againft the truth of the account I have given. Similar degeneracies have prevailed in other inftances of no lefs importance.

Reafon in man, like the will of the community in the political world, was intended to give law to his whole conduct, and to be the fupreme controuling power within him. The paffions are fubordinate powers, or an *executive force* under the direction of reafon, kindly given to be, as it were, wind and tide to the veffel of life in its courfe through this world to future honour and felicity.——How different from this is the *actual* ftate of man?——Thofe powers which were deftined to *govern* are made to *ferve*; and thofe powers which were deftined to *ferve*, are allowed to *govern*. Paffion guides human life; and moft

---

. (*a*) See Remarks on the Acts of the Thirteenth Parliament of *Great Britain*. P. 34, &c.——" Is not the fame reafoning " applicable to taxes paid for the fupport of civil government? " Are not thefe too the property of the civil magiftrate?" Ibid. p. 56.——If I underftand this writer, his meaning is, not only that the taxes which the civil magiftrate *has* impofed are his property; but alfo, *any* which he fhall pleafe to impofe.

men make no other ufe of their reafon than to juftify whatever their intereft or their inclinations determine them to do.

RELIGION likewife (the perfection of REASON) is, in its true nature, the infpirer of humanity and joy, and the fpring of all that can be great and worthy in a character; and were we to fee its genuine effects among mankind, we fhould fee nothing but peace and hope and juftice and kindnefs, founded on that regard to God and to his will, which is the nobleft principle of action.— But how different an afpect does religion actually wear? What is it, too generally, in the practice of mankind, but a gloomy and cruel fuperftition, rendering them fevere and four; teaching them to compound for wickednefs by punctuality in religious forms; and prompting them to harrafs, perfecute and exterminate one another?

The fame perverfion has taken place ftill more remarkably in CHRISTIANITY; the perfection of RELIGION.—JESUS CHRIST has eftablifhed among Chriftians an abfolute equality. He has declared, that they have but *one* mafter, even himfelf; and that they are all *brethren*; and, therefore, has commanded them not to be called *mafters*; and, inftead of affuming authority over one another, to be ready to *wafh one another's feet* (a). The

(a) Matth. xxiii. 8—12.——John xiii. 14.

princes

princes of the Gentiles, he says, exercise lordship over them, and are flattered with (*a*) high titles; but he has ordained, that it shall not be so amongst his followers; and that if any one of them would be *chief*, he must be the *servant* of all.——The clergy in his church are, by his appointment, no more than a body of men, chosen by the different societies of Christians, to conduct their worship, and to promote their spiritual improvement, without any other powers than those of persuasion and instruction. It is expressly directed, that they shall not make themselves Lordsof *God's heritage*, or exercise dominion over the faith of Christians, but be *helpers of their joy* (*b*).——Who can, without astonishment, compare these appointments of Christianity, with the events which have happened in the Christian church?——That religion which thus inculcates humility and forbids all domination, and the end of which was to produce *peace on earth, and good-will among men*, has been turned into an occasion of animosities the most dreadful, and of ambition the most destructive. Notwithstanding its mildness and benignity, and the tendency it has to extinguish in the human breast pride and malevolence; it has been the means of arming the spirits of men with unrelenting fury

(*a*) Luke xxii. 25, &c. · (*b*) 1 Pet. v. 3.——2 Cor. i. 24.

against one another. Instead of *peace*, it has brought a *sword*; and its professors, instead of washing one another's feet, have endeavoured to tread on one another's necks.——The ministers, in particular, of Christianity, became, soon after its establishment, an independent body of spiritual rulers, nominating one another in perpetual succession; claiming, by divine right, the highest powers; and forming a HIERARCHY, which by degrees produced a despotism more extravagant than any that ever before existed on this earth.

A considerate person must find difficulties in enquiring into the causes and reasons of that depravity of human nature which has produced these evils, and rendered the best institutions liable to be so corrupted. This enquiry is much the same with the enquiry into the origin of moral evil, which has in all ages puzzled human wisdom. I have at present nothing to do with it. It is enough for my purpose in these observations, that the facts I have mentioned prove undeniably, that the state of civil government in the world affords no reason for concluding, that I have not given a just account of its true nature and origin.

I have shewn at the beginning of this section, that it is free government alone that can preserve from oppression, give security to the rights of a

people,

people, and answer the ends of government. It is necessary I should here observe, that I would not be understood to mean, that there can be no *kind* or *degree* of security for the rights of a people, under any government which cannot be denominated free. Even under an absolute Monarchy or an Aristrocracy, there may be laws and customs which, having gained sacredness by time, may restrain oppression, and afford some important securities.——Under governments by representation, there must be still greater checks on oppression, provided the representation, though partial, is uncorrupt, and also frequently changed. In these circumstances, there may be so much of a common interest between the body of representatives and the people, and they may stand so much on one ground, that there will be no temptations to oppression.——The taxes which the representative body impose, they will be obliged themselves to pay; and the laws they make, they will make with the prospect of soon returning to the situation of those for whom they make them, and of being themselves governed by them.

It seems particularly worth notice here, that as far as there are any such checks under any government, they are the consequence of its partaking so far of Liberty, and that the security attending them is more or less in proportion as a government partakes more or less of Liberty.

If, under an absolute government, fundamental laws and long established institutions give security in any instances, it is because they are held so sacred that a despot is afraid to violate them; or, in other words, because a people, not being completely subdued, have still some controul over the government.——The like is more evidently true under mixed governments of which a house of representatives, fairly chosen and freely deliberating and resolving, forms a part; and it is one of the highest recommendations of such governments that, even when the representation is most imperfect, they have a tendency to give more security than any other governments.—— Under other governments, it is the fear of exciting insurrections by contradicting established maxims, that restrains oppression. But, as, in general, a people will bear much, and are seldom driven to resistance till grievances become intolerable, their rulers can venture far without danger; and therefore, under such governments, are very imperfectly restrained. On the contrary; If there is an honest representation, vested with powers like to those of our *House of Commons*, the redress of grievances, as soon as they appear, will be always easily attainable, and the rulers of a state will be under a necessity of regarding the first beginnings of discontent.—Such, and greater than can be easily described, are the advantages

of

of even an *imperfect representation* in a government. How great then muft be the bleffing of a COMPLETE REPRESENTATION?——(a) It is this only gives full fecurity; and that can properly denominate a people free.

It deferves to be added here, that as there can be no private character fo abandoned as to want *all* virtue; fo there can be no government fo flavifh, as to exclude *every* reftraint upon oppreffion.——The moft flavifh and, therefore, the worft governments are thofe under which there is nothing to fet bounds to oppreffion, befides the *difcretion* and *humanity* of thofe who govern.—— Of this kind are the following governments.

Firft, All governments *purely* defpotic. Thefe may be either monarchical, or ariftocratical. The latter are the worft, agreeably to a common obfervation, that it is better to have *one* mafter than *many*. The appetites of a fingle defpot may be eafily fatiated; but this may be impoffible where there is a multitude.

Secondly, All provincial governments.—The hiftory of mankind proves thefe to be the worft of all governments; and that no oppreffion is equal

(a) He who wants to be convinced of the *practicability*, even in this country, of a complete reprefentation, fhould read a pamphlet lately publifhed, the title of which is, TAKE YOUR CHOICE.

to that which one people are capable of practising towards another. I have mentioned some of the reasons of this in the *Observations on Civil Liberty*, Part I. sect. 3. Bodies of men do not feel for one another as individuals do. The *odium* of a cruel action, when shared among many, is not regarded. The master of slaves working on a plantation, though he may keep them down to prevent their becoming strong enough to emancipate themselves, yet is led by *interest*, as well as *humanity*, to govern them with such moderation, as to preserve their use: But these causes will produce more of this good effect, when the slaves are under the eye of their proprietor, and form a part of his family, than when they are settled on a distant plantation, where he can know little of them, and is obliged to trust them to the management of rapacious servants.

It is particularly observable here, that *free* governments, though happier in themselves, are more oppressive to their provinces than despotic governments. Or, in other words, that the *subjects* of free (*a*) states are worse slaves than the subjects of states not free. This is one of the observations which Mr. HUME represents as an universal axiom in politicks (*b*).——" Though,

(*a*) " A *free* subject of a free state" is a contradiction in terms. See the Proclamation for a Fast.

(*b*) Mr. Hume's Essays. Vol. i. Essay iv. p. 31.

" says

"says he, free governments have been commonly the moſt happy for thoſe who partake of their freedom, yet are they the moſt oppreſſive and ruinous to their provinces; and this obſervation may be fixed as an univerſal axiom in politics. What cruel tyrants were the Romans over the world during the time of their commonwealth? ——After the diſſolution of the commonwealth the Roman yoke became eaſier upon the provinces, as *Tacitus* informs us; and it may be obſerved, that many of the worſt Emperors (*Domitian*, for inſtance) were very careful to prevent all oppreſſion of the provinces.—— The oppreſſion and tyranny of the *Carthaginians* over their ſubject ſtates in *Africa* went ſo far, as we learn from *Polybius* (Lib. 1. cap. 72.) that not content with exacting the *half* of all the produce of the ground, which of itſelf was a very high rent, they alſo loaded them with many other taxes.—If we paſs from antient to modern times we ſhall always find the obſervation to hold. The provinces of abſolute monarchies are always better treated than thoſe of free ſtates."

Thirdly, Among the worſt ſorts of governments I reckon all governments by a corrupt repreſentation.——There is no inſtance in which the trite obſervation is more true than in this, "that the beſt things when corrupted become the "worſt."

"worst." A corrupt representation is so far from being any *defence* against oppression, that it is a *support* to it. Long established customs, in this case, afford no security, because, under the sanction of such a representation, they may be easily undermined or counteracted; nor is there any injury to a people which, with the help of such an instrument, may not be committed with safety. It is not, however, every degree of corruption, that will destroy the use of a representation, and turn it into an evil so dreadful. In order to this, corruption must pass a certain limit. But *every degree* of it *tends* to this, saps the foundation of Liberty, and poisons the fountain of Legislation. And when it gets to its last stage, and has proceeded its utmost length: When, in particular, the means by which candidates get themselves chosen are such as admit the *worst*, but exclude the *best* men; a House of Representatives becomes little better than a sink into which is collected all that is most worthless and vile in a kingdom.—— There cannot be a greater calamity than such a government.——It is impossible there should be a condition more wretched than that of a nation, once free, so degenerated.

CONCLUSION.

IT is time to difmifs this fubject. But I cannot take a final leave of it, (and probably of all fubjects of this kind) without adding the following reflections on our own ftate in this kingdom.

It is well known, that MONTESQUIEU has paid the higheſt compliment to this country, by defcribing its conſtitution of government, in giving an account of a perfect government; and by drawing the character of its inhabitants, in giving an account of the manners and characters of a free people.——
" All (he fays) having, in free ſtates, a ſhare in
" government, and the laws not being made for
" fome more than others, they confider themſelves
" as *monarchs*, and are more properly *confederates*
" *than fellow-fubjects*.——No one citizen being
" fubject to another, each fets a greater value on
" his Liberty than on the glory of any of his fel-
" low-citizens.——Being independent, they are
" proud; for the pride of kings is founded on
" their independence.——They are in a conſtant
" ferment, and believe themſelves in danger,
" even in thofe moments when they are moſt
" fafe.——They reafon; but it is indifferent whe-
" ther they reafon well or ill. It is fufficient
" that

"that they *do* reason. Hence springs that Li-
"berty which is their security.——This state,
"however, will lose its Liberty. It will perish,
"when the *Legiſlative* power shall become more
"corrupt than the *executive.*" (*a*)

Such is the account which this great writer gave, many years ago, of the *British* constitution and people. We may learn from it, that we have nothing to fear from that disposition to examine every public measure, to censure ministers of state, and to be restless and clamorous, which has hitherto characterized us.——On the contrary; we shall have every thing to fear, when this disposition is lost. As soon as a people grow secure, and cease to be quick in taking alarms, they are undone. A free constitution of government cannot be preserved without an earnest and unremitting jealousy. Our Constitution, in particular, is so excellent, that it is the properest object of such a jealousy. For my own part, I admire so much the general frame and principles of it, that I could be almost satisfied with that representation of the kingdom, which forms the most important part of it, had I no other objection to this representation than its *inadequateneſs*. Did it consist of a body of men, fairly elected for a short term, by a number of independent persons, of all orders in every part of the king-

(*a*) Spirit of Laws. Book xix. ch. 27.

dom,

dom, equal to the number of the prefent voters; and were it, after being elected, under no undue influence; it would be a fecurity of fuch importance, that I fhould be lefs difpofed to complain of the injuftice done, by its inadequatenefs, to the greateft part of the kingdom by depriving them of one their natural and unalienable rights. To fuch a body of reprefentatives we might commit, with confidence, the guardianfhip of our rights, knowing, that having one intereft with the reft of the ftate, they could not violate them; or that if they ever did, a little time would bring the power of gaining redrefs without tumult or violence.——Happy the people fo bleffed.—— If wife, they will endeavour, by every poffible method, to preferve the purity of their reprefentation; and, fhould it have degenerated, they will lofe no time in effecting a reformation of it.—— But if, unhappily, infection fhould have pervaded the whole mafs of the ftate, and there fhould be no room to hope for any reformation, it will be ftill fome confolation to reflect, that flavery, in all its rigour, will not immediately follow. Between the time in which the fecurities of Liberty are undermined, and its final fubverfion, there is commonly a flattering interval during which the *enjoyment* of Liberty may be continued, in confequence of fundamental laws and rooted habits which cannot be at once exterminated. And this interval

interval is longer or shorter, according as the progress of corruption is more or less rapid; and men in power more or less attentive to improve favourable opportunities. —— The government of this country, in particular, is so well balanced, and the institutions of our common law are so admirable, and have taken such deep root, that we can bear much decay before our liberties fall. ——Fall, however, they must, if our public affairs do not soon take a new turn. That very evil, which, according to the great writer I have quoted, is to produce our ruin, we see working every where and increasing every day.——The following facts, among many others, shew too plainly whither we are tending and how far we are advanced.

First. It seems to me, that a general indifference is gaining ground fast among us.——This is the necessary effect of increasing luxury and dissipation; but there is another cause of it, which I think of with particular regret.—In consequence of having been often duped by false patriots; and found, that the leaders of opposition, when they get into places, forget all their former declarations; the nation has been led to a conviction, that all patriotism is imposture, and all opposition to the measures of government nothing but a struggle for power and its emoluments. The honest and independent part of the nation entertain at present

most

most of this conviction; and, therefore, having few public men to whom they can look with confidence, they give up all zeal, and sink into inactivity and despondence.

Secondly. At the Revolution, the House of Commons acquired its just weight in the constitution; and, for some years afterwards, it was often giving much trouble to men in power. Of late, it is well known, that means have been tryed and a system adopted for quieting it.——I will not say with what success———But I must say, that the men whose policy this has been, have struck at the very *heart* of public liberty, and are the worst traitors this kingdom ever saw.——" If ever,
" (says Judge *Blackstone*) it should happen, that
" the independency of any one of the three
" branches of our legislature should be lost; or
" that it should become subservient to the views
" of either of the other two, there would soon be
" an end of our constitution. The legislature
" would be changed from that which was origi-
" nally set up by the general consent and funda-
" mental act of the society; and such a change,
" however effected, is according to Mr. *Locke*
" (who perhaps carries his theory too far) at
" once an entire dissolution of the bands of
" government, and the people are thereby
" reduced to a state of anarchy, with liberty
" to

" to conſtitute to themſelves a new legiſlative
" power." (a)

Thirdly. Soon after the REVOLUTION, bills for triennial parliaments paſſed both Houſes, in oppoſition to the court (b). At the ACCESSION, ſeptennial parliaments were eſtabliſhed. Since this laſt period, many attempts have been made, by the friends of the conſtitution, to reſtore triennial parliaments; and, formerly, it was not without difficulty that the miniſtry were able to defeat theſe attempts. The diviſion in the Houſe of Commons in 1735, on a bill for this purpoſe, was 247 to 184.——I need not ſay, that *now* all ſuch attempts drop of themſelves. So much are the ſentiments of our repreſentatives changed in this inſtance, that the motion for ſuch a bill, annually made by a worthy member of the Houſe of Commons, can ſcarcely produce a ſerious debate, or gain the leaſt attention.———For ſeveral years, at the beginning of the laſt reign, the HOUSE OF COMMONS conſtantly paſſed *penſion* and *place* bills, which were as conſtantly rejected by the HOUSE OF LORDS. At preſent, no one is ſo romantic as ever to think of introducing any ſuch bills into the Houſe of Commons.

(a) Introduction to the Commentaries on the Laws of England, p. 48. See alſo Book i. ch. 8.

(b) In 1692 King William rejected a bill for triennial Parliaments, after it had paſſed both Houſes. But in a following year he thought proper to give his aſſent to it.

Fourthly,

Fourthly. Standing armies have in all ages been deſtructive to the Liberties of the ſtates into which they have been admitted.—MONTESQUIEU (*a*) obſerves, that the preſervation of Liberty in ENGLAND requires, that it ſhould have no land forces.——Dr. FERGUSON calls the eſtabliſhment of ſtanding armies "A FATAL REFINEMENT in " the preſent ſtate of civil government." (*b*)—— Mr. *Hume* pronounces " our ſtanding army a " mortal diſtemper in the Britiſh conſtitution, of " which it muſt *inevitably* periſh." (*c*)—Formerly, the nation was apprehenſive of this danger; and the *ſtanding army* was a conſtant ſubject of warm debate in both Houſes of Parliament. The principal reaſon then aſſigned for continuing it was, the ſecurity of the Houſe of HANOVER againſt the friends of the *Pretender*. This is a reaſon which now exiſts no more; the Houſe of *Hanover* being ſo well eſtabliſhed as not to want any ſuch ſecurity.——The ſtanding army alſo is now more numerous and formidable than ever; and yet all oppoſition to it is loſt, and it is become in a manner a part of the conſtitution.

Fifthly. For many years after the acceſſion the national debt was thought an evil ſo alarming, that the reduction of it was recommended every

(*a*) Spirit of Laws. Book xix. ch. 27.
(*b*) Hiſtory of Civil Society. Part vi. ſect. 5.
(*c*) *Political* Diſcourſes. Eſſay xii. p. 301.

year from the throne to the attention of Parliament as an object of the laſt importance. The FUND appropriated to this purpoſe was called the ONLY HOPE of the kingdom; and when the practice of alienating it begun, it was reckoned a kind of ſacrilege, and zealouſly oppoſed in the Houſe of *Commons*, and proteſted againſt in the Houſe of *Lords*. But now, though the debt is almoſt *tripled*, we ſit under it with perfect indifference; and the ſacred fund, which repeated laws had ordered to be applied *to no other purpoſe* than the redemption of it, is always alienated of courſe, and become a conſtant part of the current ſupplies, and much more an encouragement to diſſipation than a preſervative from bankruptcy.

Sixthly. Nothing is more the duty of the repreſentatives of a nation than to keep a ſtrict eye over the expenditure of the money granted for public ſervices.—In the reign of King William, the Houſe of Commons paſſed almoſt every year bills for appointing commiſſioners for taking, ſtating and examining the public accounts; and, particularly, the army and navy debts and contracts. In the reign of Queen Ann ſuch bills became leſs frequent. But ſince the acceſſion, only two motions have been made for ſuch bills; one in 1715, and the other in 1741; and both were rejected.

Seventhly.

Seventhly. I hope I may add, that there was a time when the kingdom could not have been brought to acquiesce in what was done in the case of the *Middlesex* election. This is a precedent which, by giving the House of Commons the power of excluding its members at discretion, and of introducing others in their room on a minority of votes, has a tendency to make it a self-created House, and to destroy entirely the right of representation: And a few more such precedents would completely overthrow the constitution.

Lastly. I cannot help mentioning here the addition which has been lately made to the power of the Crown, by throwing into its hands the *East-India Company*. Nothing more unfavourable to the security of public Liberty has been done since the REVOLUTION: And should our statesmen, thus strengthened by the patronage of the EAST, be farther strengthened by the conquest and patronage of the WEST, they will indeed have no small reason for triumph; and there will be little left to protect us against the encroachments and usurpations of power. ROME sunk into slavery, in consequence of enlarging its territories, and becoming the center of the wealth of conquered provinces, and the seat of universal empire. It seems the appointment of Providence, that free states, when, not contented with *self*-government, and prompted by the love of domination, they make themselves masters of other states, shall lose Liberty at the same time that they take it away; and, by subduing, be themselves subdued. Distant and dependent provinces can be governed only by a military force. And a military force which governs abroad, will soon govern at home. The *Romans* were so sensible of this, that they made it treason for any of their generals to march their armies over the *Rubicon* into *Italy*. CÆSAR, therefore, when he came to this river, hesitated; but he passed it, and enslaved his country.

" Among the circumstances (says Dr. FERGU-
" SON) which in the event of national prosperity
" and in the result of commercial arts, lead to
" the establishment of despotism, there is none
" perhaps that arrives at this termination with so
" sure an aim as the perpetual enlargement of ter-
" ritory. In every state the freedom of its mem-
" bers depends on the balance and adjustment of
" its interior parts; and the existence of any such
" freedom among mankind depends on the ba-
" lance of nations. In the progress of conquest
" those who are subdued are said to have lost their
" liberties. But, from the history of mankind,
" to conquer or to be conquered has appeared in
" effect the same." (*a*)

(*a*) History of Civil Society. Part iv. sect. 5.

Many

Many more facts of this kind might eafily be enumerated; but thefe are fufficient.——They fhew, with fad evidence, how faft we have, for fome time, been advancing towards the greateft of all public calamities.

We may, alfo, infer from the preceding obfervations, that there is only one way in which our deliverance is poffible; and that is, by RESTORING OUR GRAND NATIONAL SECURITY. This is the object which our great men in oppofition ought to hold forth to the kingdom, and to bind themfelves by fome decifive tefts to do all they can to obtain. That patriotifm muft be fpurious which does not carry its views principally to this. Without it, nothing is of great importance to the kingdom; and even an accommodation with *America* would only preferve a limb, and fave from prefent danger, while a gangrene was left to confume the vitals.

But, probably, we are gone too far; and corruption has ftruck its roots too deep to leave us much room for hope.——Mr. HUME has obferved, (*a*) that as the affairs of this country are not likely to take a turn favourable to the eftablifhment of a perfect plan of Liberty, " an ab-
" folute monarchy is the eafieft death, the true
" EUTHANASIA of the Britifh conftitution."—

(*a*) See Mr. Hume's Effays. Vol. i. p. 91.

If this obfervation is juft, our conftitution (fhould no great calamity intervene) is likely, in fome future period, to receive a very quiet diffolution.——At prefent, however, it muft be acknowledged, that we enjoy a degree of Liberty, civil and religious, which has feldom been paralleled among mankind. We ought to rejoice in this happinefs; and to be grateful to that benevolent difpofer of all events who bleffes us with it. But, at the fame time, our hearts muft bleed when we reflect, that, the fupports of it having given way, it is little more than a *fufferance* which we owe to the temper of the times; the lenity of our governors; and fome awe, in which the friends of defpotifm are ftill held, by the voice and fpirit of the uncorrupted part of the kingdom.———May thefe caufes, if no better fecurities can be hoped for, long delay our fate.

It muft not be forgotten, that all I have now faid is meant on the fuppofition, that our affairs will proceed fmoothly till, by a common and natural progrefs, we have gone the round of other nations once free, and are brought to their end.———But it is poffible this may not happen.——— Our circumftances are fingular; and give us reafon to fear, that we have before us a death which will not be eafy or common.

PART

PART II.

CONTAINING

REMARKS on some Particulars in a SPEECH at opening the BUDGET in *April* 1776.

SECT. I.

Supplemental Observations on the Surplus of the Revenue; the Quantity of Coin in the Kingdom; and Paper-Credit.

IT is well known, that the great minister who presides over our finances, took occasion, at opening the Budget in April last, to enter into a particular account of the state of the nation. In this account, he represented us as in a condition the most sound and happy; our trade and revenue flourishing; our common people well provided for; our debts and taxes light; our current specie sufficiently ample; our paper-circulation safe; and the BANK, in particular, as little less firm and durable than the world.

This account, so encouraging and flattering, was generally underſtood to be given in deſigned oppoſition to another account very different, which had been given in the *Obſervations on Civil Liberty*.----It cannot, therefore, I hope, be thought too preſuming in me to offer the following remarks in my own defence.

I have grounded my opinion of the hazardous ſtate of the kingdom, partly on the ſmallneſs of the ſurplus in the revenue, and the nature and circumſtances of our paper-circulation, compared with the quantity of *ſpecie* in the kingdom, and the weight of our debts and taxes.

The ſurplus of the revenue I have made out in two different methods; and by a deduction ſo minute, that it is, I think, ſcarcely poſſible it ſhould be materially wrong. One of theſe methods brings it out 338,759*l. per ann.* (*a*): and the other, 300,000*l. per ann.* ſuppoſing the expence of calling in the gold coin, and the profits of lotteries excluded; the land-tax at three ſhillings in the pound; and the peace eſtabliſhment the ſame that it has been at a medium for eleven years, from 1764 to 1775.

Nothing more was ſaid in oppoſition to this, than a general intimation, that had it not been for the war with *America*, the peace-eſtabliſhment for

(*a*) See the concluſion of the Third Part.

the

the navy would have been reduced, and a sufficient surplus gained (including lotteries) to enable parliament to pay off a million every year of the public debt.

I am very sensible that reductions of the public expences and improvements in the revenue are practicable, which would give such a surplus. But I am afraid, they will never take place. Nor can I think it proper, in determining what permanent surplus we possess, to include those pernicious profits of lotteries, by which infinitely more is upon the whole lost than gained; or, to form our judgment of the expence of *future* years, by any other rule than the medium expence of *past* years. ——It would, however, give little consolation, were there a certainty that, had peace continued, a MILLION annually of the public debt would have been discharged. This would have made a very slow progress in discharging our debts. A million every year discharged in peace, and eight or ten millions every year added in war, would leave us under the necessity of breaking at last. But hitherto we have not proceeded in a course so favourable. The great person to whom I refer, must know, that in 1772, he announced in the *House of Commons*, his intention to pay off a *million and a half* every year, and SEVENTEEN MILLIONS in ten years; that yet only £.800,000*l.* was paid off in the three subsequent years; and that,

that, on account of the increase of the *navy* and *civil-list* debts, there has not been in fact the ability (without the help of lotteries) to pay half that sum.

In page 74th of the *Observations on Civil Liberty*, I have said, " that it has appeared lately, " that the gold specie of the kingdom, is no " more than about TWELVE MILLIONS AND A " HALF."——This assertion has been much controverted; and it is therefore necessary I should give a distinct account of the reasons on which it was grounded.

I had learnt from unquestionable authority, that the quantity of gold coin brought into the mint, by the Acts of Parliament and Proclamations in 1773 and 1774, was about NINE MILLIONS (*a*); or as much as, when recoined, amounted nearly to that sum.——I find also, that it was expected by the best judges, that the proclamation lately issued would bring in about *three* millions. These two sums make up *twelve* millions; and they include the gold coin of *Ireland*. Let this be estimated at a (*b*) million; and the whole gold coin

---

(*a*) This was confirmed by the account of the noble Lord at opening the last Budget.

(*b*) I have mentioned this sum at random. It is not of great consequence whether it is half a million too little or half a million too much.

of *Britain*, to be brought in by all the calls, will be ELEVEN millions; and none will remain, except that part which was deficient lefs than a grain in a guinea, and remained in the kingdom, at the time the coin Act took effect in June 1773. We are here left entirely to conjecture. But it fhould be remembered, that for many years before 1773, the heavy coin was catched up as foon as iffued, and either clipped, or melted down and exported; and that from hence arofe fuch a fcarcity of heavy coin, that, in fome counties, heavy guineas might be difpofed of at a premium.——In fuch circumftances, an allowance of about a million and a half, for the coin deficient lefs than a grain in a guinea before the coin Act in 1773, feems to be fufficient; and therefore, it might, I think, with reafon be faid, that it appeared that the gold coin of the kingdom was about TWELVE MILLIONS AND A HALF.

But there is another reafon, by which I have been convinced, that this is a moderate eftimate.

The quantity of gold coin, deficient between three and fix grains in a guinea, was 4.800,000*l.* and this, when recoined, made 4.600,000*l.*—— The coin deficient lefs than three grains could not have been fo much, for the following reafons. Firft, new coin being rougher, wears fafter than old coin; and therefore, does not remain fo long in in any given degree of deficiency.—Secondly, coin, deficient lefs than three grains, is fubject to feveral peculiar caufes of diminution and deftruction.— Clipping and fweating remove part of it to greater degrees of deficiency; and part is deftroyed by being melted down and exported; whereas, lighter coin is diminifhed only by being worn (*a*).

(*a*) The quantity of coin within all equal degrees of deficiency would be equal, were equal quantities iffued every year, and were there alfo no caufe which diminifhed or deftroyed it, except the *uniform* operation of time in wearing it. Any caufe, therefore, which deftroys it more, or diminifhes it fafter at firft than at laft, muft render the quantity lefs in the firft degrees of deficiency. And the fame muft be the confequence of a greater proportion iffued formerly, in any given time, than of late.——The caufes of diminution never probably operated fo much on the gold coin as they did for about twelve years before 1773; and this will balance the greater proportion coined during that time. The very reafon of the increafe of coinage in thofe years was, a neceffity created by the lofs of the new coin, and never before felt in an equal degree. The coinage, however, in thofe years, was not fo much more than ufual as fome may imagine. In ten years before 1770, eight millions and a half were coined; and in twelve years after the *Acceffion*, the fame quantity was coined; and in twenty-feven years after the *Acceffion*, more was coined than in twenty-feven years before 1770. See *Confiderations on Money, Bullion*, &c. p. 2.——The whole quantity of gold coined from the Acceffion to 1770, was near 29 millions; more than one half of which muft have been melted and exported; and, the greateft part of the remainder muft have been precipitated in its progrefs towards deficiency by being clipped and fweated.

Thefe

These reasons seem to prove, that if the gold coin, deficient in June 1773 less than three grains, is estimated at *five millions*, (that is, at a little more than the coin deficient between three and six grains) it will be rated rather too high; and the conclusion will be, that the whole of our gold coin (exclusive of the *Irish*) might possibly be *less*, but could not have been *much more*, than the sum at which I have reckoned it.

Such have been the facts and arguments by which my judgment has been determined in this instance.——But it must not be overlooked, that it helps only to ascertain the quantity of *circulating* specie in the kingdom, as distinguished from that which is *hoarded*. When the *Observations on Civil Liberty* were published, I did not apprehend, that this part of the coin could be considerable enough to deserve regard. But the contrary has lately appeared. The Proclamation issued last summer, and which it was expected would bring in about three millions, has, I am informed, brought in about *six millions and a half*. This exceeds the sum at which I have been led to state the *whole* gold coin deficient less than three grains; and proves, that several millions must have been hoarded *(a)*. Nor, I think,

---

(*a*) When the silver *specie* was recoined in King William's time, it appeared, that a great treasure had been hoarded before

I think, will this appear incredible, when it is recollected, that only gold coin under three grains of deficiency is likely to be hoarded; and also, that diftruft of the *Funds* and of Paper-money has a particular tendency to increafe the practice of hoarding.

Affifted, therefore, by this new light, I would now ftate the *circulating* gold coin of the kingdom before 1773, nearly as I did before; and call it TWELVE or THIRTEEN MILLIONS. But the whole gold coin (including the hoarded part) I would reckon at SIXTEEN or SEVENTEEN MILLIONS (*b*).

An account very different from this was given at opening the Budget; the fubftance of which I will ftate as faithfully as my memory will enable me; and juft as I underftood it.

"From the beginning of the year 1772, to
"the 23d of April laft, 13.200,000*l.* had been
"coined at the Tower; and on that day there
"was 600,000*l.* more ready to be coined.——

before the *Revolution*, in confequence of the danger of public liberty at that time. See Davenant's Works, Vol. I. p. 439, &c.

In *Ruffia* it is reckoned, that as much money lies buried under ground, as exifts above ground.

(*b*) In thefe fums is included all the coin which the late Proclamations have brought in from HOLLAND and other foreign countries; and which, I think, ought not to be deemed a part of the refting ftock of the kingdom.

All

" All this, (it was intimated) is now left in the
" kingdom. The laſt Proclamation, it was ex-
" pected, would bring in three millions more;
" which, added to the coin deficient leſs than a
" grain reſting in the kingdom at the time of the
" Coin Act in 1773, and iſſued before 1772,
" will make the whole, EIGHTEEN OR NINETEEN
" MILLIONS (*a*)."

On this account I would obſerve,

Firſt. That if juſt, it proves that, in 1773, a *third* at leaſt of the *circulating* coin was in the beſt ſtate poſſible. For the late calls having ſhewn, that there was then, in *Britain* and *Ireland*, no more than about twelve *millions* deficient *more* than a grain; ſix millions (that is, a third of eighteen millions) or ſeven millions (that is, more than a third of nineteen millions) muſt have been deficient *leſs* than a grain. (*b*)—It will alſo follow,

(*a*) Or deducting a million for the *Iriſh* coin, ſeventeen or eighteen millions.

(*b*) This is ſaid on the ſuppoſition, that the laſt call would bring in no more than was expected, or about three millions. Its having brought in above double this ſum makes little difference. For it proves, that the whole quantity of gold coin muſt have been (according to Lord NORTH's method of computing) 21 or 22 millions; and the quantity deficient more than a grain about 15 millions; and, conſequently, ſix or ſeven millions (that is, near a *third*) will ſtill remain to be the quantity deficient leſs than a grain.

(ſince

(since the quantity brought in by the first call is known to have been 4,900,000 l.) that but little more than a *fourth* could have been deficient so much as six grains, or a shilling in a guinea.—— No person can think this credible who recollects the distress of traffic, and the complaints of the kingdom before 1773.

Secondly. The truth of the account I have stated depends, in a great measure, on the supposition, that all the gold coined since the beginning of 1772 is now in the kingdom. I cannot conceive on what grounds this was taken for granted.——From the beginning of 1772 to June 1773, the practice of clipping was more prevalent than it had ever been. During the greatest part of 1772, the price of gold was so much above mint price, that a profit, from 2 to 4 *per cent.* might be got by melting heavy guineas *a*). And, in February in that year, the price of gold was at

---

(*a*) It has been thought very strange, that a piece of metal should bear a higher price, merely because it wants the stamp of the mint. But the reason is, that bullion alone being exportable in any considerable quantity, the price of it must vary as the demand for it varies; or, in other words, as the *balance of payment* between us and the rest of the world is favourable or unfavourable.——This will be explained at the beginning of the Third Part, where it will appear that, in consequence of the increase of luxury and the national debt, this balance has been generally against us ever since the end of the last war.

4 l. 1 s.

4l. 1s. 6d. per ounce; and 4 $\frac{1}{2}$ *per cent.* might be got by melting heavy guineas. Instead, therefore, of believing, that all the gold coined since the beginning of 1772 remains with us; I think it almost certain, that the greatest part of all coined during the first year and a half of this period, has been either clipped or melted into bullion. That part which was clipped has been recoined; and that part which was melted has been either recoined or exported; and, therefore, neither has made any addition to the coin of the kingdom.

These observations demonstrate, that the amount of the gold coin at the time of the Coin Act in 1773, must have been near the sum at which I have reckoned it. There may, for ought I know, have been an increase since; but I shall not believe there has, till I know, whether the coin brought in by the last proclamation has been all recoined and issued. But this cannot be expected; for should it be done, FOUR MILLIONS (*a*) more will have been coined and issued, than has been brought in.——The truth, therefore, may be, that the coinage, since June 1773, has been car-

(*a*) The coin brought in last Summer, added to near 14 millions coined from the beginning of 1772 to the time of the last call, amounts to about 20 millions and a half; but only 16 millions and a half have been brought in, including the coin from *Ireland* and foreign countries.

ried on only to provide a supply of new coin to be exchanged for old; in which case, the quantity of coin in the kingdom, even according to this method of computing it, will come out nearly the same with that which I have given.

After all, let the *specie* of the kingdom, including the silver, be allowed to be as considerable as some have asserted; or about four millions more than I have reckoned it; the difference arising from hence will not be of particular consequence; and it will be still true, that notwithstanding all our increase of trade and apparent opulence, the *specie* of the kingdom (*a*) is not much more than it was at the *Revolution.*——What then is all the rest of our circulating cash? What is it keeps up rents; feeds our luxury; pays our taxes; supplies the revenue, and supports government? —Paper, chiefly, emitted, not only at the Bank, but by tradesmen, merchants, and bankers in every corner of the kingdom.——And is this a solid

(*a*) Or EIGHTEEN MILLIONS AND A HALF. See Dr. DAVENANT's Works, Vol. i. p. 363, &c. 443, &c. A great part of this specie was carried out of the nation in King WILLIAM's wars; and the consequence was, that the taxes became unproductive; and that Government fell under great difficulties, from which it was afterwards relieved by the establishment of the *Bank* and the increase of trade. See the beginning of the Third Part.

and permanent support? (*b*) Is there, in the annals of the world, another instance of a great kingdom so supported?———The causes are numberless which may suddenly destroy it; and were

this

(*b*) The paper currency of the Colonies is one of the greatest disadvantages under which they labour; but it is of a more safe and permanent nature than ours. Were it not so, it could not have been of the least use to them for the last year and a half. He who doubts this, need only consider what our paper would be worth were we now invaded as they are.

This difference depends chiefly, on the following circumstances.———Their paper is not payable on demand.—It is a legal tender.———It represents fixed property which is mortgaged for it.———It does not support such a monstrous debt as ours.—And when public emergencies require any extraordinary emissions, they are generally sunk by taxes in four or five years.——— It is the first of these circumstances that gives our paper its currency; and it is also this circumstance that creates the danger attending it, by rendering it incapable of sustaining any great shock or panic.———The possession of securities equal in nominal value to the amount of the paper emitted, or the debts contracted, is of little consequence when the value of these securities depends on the paper, and is created by it; that is, in other words, when the debts themselves are the very cash which must pay the debts.———Nothing can be more unnatural than such a state of things; and it may hereafter be a curious object of enquiry, how it could be ever possible that it should subsist any long time.

In page 78 of the *Observations on Civil Liberty*, I have said, " that the kingdom of FRANCE has no such dependence as " we have on paper-credit; and that its specie amounts to " 67 millions sterling." In mentioning this sum I took the

F   lowest

this to happen, we should fall at once, with a debt of 140 millions upon us, to the state we were in before the REVOLUTION.——Imagination cannot paint to itself the shock this would give.——

lowest of different accounts which I had then received from different authorities. I have since received accounts which make it 87 millions and a half; or 2000 millions of *livres*. This, in particular, is the account of an author whom all know to be likely to be well informed on this subject; I mean the author of the Treatise on the *Legiflation* and *Commerce of Corn*, Part I. chap. v.——In the fame treatife it is faid, (Part I. chap. viii,) that it appears, from the returns made by the intendants of the different Provinces, that the number of *annual* deaths in the whole kingdom of France, for three years ended in 1772, was 780,040. I have been informed by the ingenious author, that this account may be depended on; and if fo, *France* must contain 26 millions of inhabitants; for the best observations prove, that no more than a thirty-third part of a whole kingdom dies annually. See Observations on Reversionary Payments, page 200.—In *Sweden*, though a nineteenth part die in the capital every year, only a thirty-fifth part die in the whole kingdom. See Philosophical Transactions, Vol. lxv. for 1775, p. 426. The particulars now mentioned, added to the nature of the debts of FRANCE as mentioned in page 78 of the *Obfervations on Civil Liberty*, form a striking contrast between the state of that kingdom and ours. Nothing gives us our superiority but the advantages we derive from our RELIGION and our LIBERTY. Even in these respects, however, they seem to be improving, while we are declining. *Montefquieu*, *Abbe Raynal*, and others of their most admired writers, inculcate principles of government, and breathe a spirit of Liberty, which, to the shame of this country, are become offensive in it.

I must

I must repeat here what I have said in the *Observations on Civil Liberty*, page 73, &c. that we should think of nothing but guarding ourselves against the danger of such a situation, by restricting our paper currency, and gradually discharging our public debts.——In giving this admonition, I look upon myself as doing my country one of the best offices in my power; and acting in the character of one who calls to another to awake who is sleeping over a precipice——But I know I call in vain.——The great minister who directs our finances has assured us all is well; and, under this persuasion, we are advancing, with unsuspicious and careless speed, to the catastrophe I have pointed out; and pursuing measures which must increase the difficulty of avoiding it, and the distress attending it.

Among these measures I have mentioned the present new coinage.——Before this coinage, I have observed, the light money always remained, because nothing could be got by melting and exporting it. But now, as soon as gold rises to the price it bore for many years before 1773, the melters and exporters of coin will be saved the trouble of selection; and every piece on which they can lay their hands will be proper for their purpose.——It seems, therefore, obvious, that, in consequence of this measure, all our coin may be carried away, and the whole superstructure of paper fupported by it, break down, before we are aware of any danger.

I will take this opportunity to add, that this meafure will at the fame time increafe our paper. This has been the confequence of the two former calls; but it will probably be more the confequence of the laft call. For, as no coin is now to be current which is more than a grain deficient; and as alfo a great deal of it is already at or near that limit; the vexation attending it will be fo intolerable, that it will be generally cried down, and paper fubftituted in its room.—— Certain it is, that nothing can prevent this evil, but another evil; I mean, the deficient coin forcing itfelf again into circulation, and furnifhing clippers with more employment than ever; and, confequently, a return, with increafed violence, of the confufion and diftrefs which took place before the Coin Act in 1773.——This, indeed, will be much the leaft of the two evils; nor, in my opinion, are there any methods of preventing the diminution of the coin, which will not produce greater evils, except fuch alterations in its form (*a*) as fhall render clipping lefs practicable, joined to the execution of fevere laws againft clippers, and a ftrict vigilance in detecting them.

Upon the whole. It feems to me, that enough had been done by the firft coin act to reftore the

(*a*). See the propofals and obfervations in a pamphlet lately publifhed by Lord Vifcount MAHON on this fubject.

gold

gold coin; and that all which has been done fince, at the expence of about 650,000 l. has been nothing but a preparation of the coin for melters and exporters, to the dreadful hazard of the kingdom.——Thefe are my prefent views of this fubject. But l muft fay, that I fufpect my own judgment in this inftance. The noble Lord, who is furnifhed with infinitely more of the means of information than I am, intimated, if I remember rightly, that there is no fuch danger: And though I did not underftand the reafon he affigned for this affertion, I muft believe, that, in a matter fo particularly interefting to the kingdom, he has gone upon the beft evidence.

SECT. II.

Of the State of the Nation; and the War with America.

AT the beginning of the preceding fection, I have taken notice of the flattering account which was given, at opening the Budget in April laft, of the ftate of the kingdom with refpect to its commerce, revenue, and opulence. On that account I fhall beg leave to offer the following reflections.

Firft. The obfervations in the laft fection prove, I think, that it is not fo well fuppotted by facts, as there is reason to wish. I am sensible, indeed, that we never made a more gay and splendid appearance. But no considerate person will draw much encouragement from hence. That pride and security; that luxury, venality and dissipation which give us this appearance, are melancholy symptoms; and have hitherto been the forerunners of distress and calamity.

Secondly. When this account was given there was a particular end to be answered by it. Additional taxes were to be imposed; and it was necessary to reconcile the public to the prospect of a great increase of its burthens, in order to carry on the war with *America*.——On other occasions, different accounts had been given. In order to prove the justice of taxing the *Americans*, the weight of our own taxes had been often insisted upon; and the difficulty of raising a sufficient force among ourselves to reduce them, had been urged as a reason for seeking and employing, at a great expence, the assistance of foreign powers. On such occasions, I have heard our unhappy and embarrassed situation mentioned; and, at the end of the last session of Parliament, one of our greatest men, whose opinion in favour of coercion, had contributed to bring us into our present situation, acknowledged the distress attending it, and represented the vessel of the state as having never before rode in so dangerous a storm.

a storm.——This is, without doubt, the truth. But, if the account on which I am remarking was just, we were then safe and happy; nor was the vessel of the state ever wafted by more gentle and prosperous gales.

But the reflection which, on this occasion, has given me most pain is the following.

If, without *America*, we can be in a state so flourishing, a war to reduce *America* must be totally inexcuseable. I wish I could engage attention to this. War is a dreadful evil; and those who involve a people in it *needlessly*, will find they have much to answer for. Nothing can ever justify it, but the necessity of it to secure some *essential* interest against unjust attacks. But, it seems, there is no interest to be secured by the present war. The revenue has never flourished so much, as since *America* has been rendered hostile to us; and it is now reckoned by many a decided point, that little depends on the *American* trade. It follows then, that if the end of the present war is to " obtain a reve- " nue," it is a revenue we do not want; if " to " maintain authority," it is an authority of no use to us.——Must not humanity shudder at such a war?——Why not let *America* alone, if we can subsist without it?——Why carry fire and sword into a happy country to do ourselves no good?

Some of the very persons who depreciate the value of the colonies, as a support to our revenue and finances, yet say, that we are now under a necessity of reducing them, or perishing. I wish such persons would give an account of the causes which, according to their ideas, create this dreadful necessity. Is it the same that led *Haman* of old to reckon all his honours and treasures nothing to him, while *Mordecai* the Jew would not bow to him?——Or, are we become so luxurious, that luxury even in the revenue is become necessary to us; and so depraved, that, like many individuals in private life, having lost *self*-dominion, we cannot subsist without dominion over *others*?

It must not be forgotten, that I speak here on the supposition, that it is possible for this country to be as safe and prosperous without *America* as some have asserted, and as was implied in what was said at opening the last Budget.——This is far from being my own opinion.—Some time or other we shall, in all probability, feel severely, in our commerce and finances, the loss of the colonies. As a source of revenue they are, I think, of great importance to us; but they are still more important as supports to our navy, and an aid to us in our wars. It appears now, that there is a force among them so formidable and so growing, that, with its assistance, any of the great *European* powers may soon make themselves masters

of

of all the *West-Indies* and *North-America*; and nothing ought to be more alarming to us than that our natural enemies fee this, and are influenced by it.——With the colonies united to us, we might be the greatest and happiest nation that ever existed. But with the colonies separated from us, and in alliance with *France* and *Spain*, we are no more a people.——They appear, therefore, to be indeed worth any price.——Our existence depends on keeping them.——But HOW are they to be kept?——Most certainly, not by forcing them to unconditional submission at the expence of many millions of money and rivers of blood. The resolution to attempt this is a melancholy instance of that infatuation, which sometimes influences the councils of kingdoms. It is attempting to keep them by a method, which, if it succeeds, will destroy their use, and make them not worth the having; and which, if it does *not* succeed, will throw them into the scale of rival powers, kindle a general war, and undo the empire.

The extension of our territories in *America*, during the last war, increased the expence of our *peace*-establishment, from 2.400,000 l. *per ann.* to four millions *per ann.*—Almost all the provinces in *America*, which used to be ours, are now to be conquered. Let the expence of this be stated at 25 or 30 millions; or, at a capital bearing a million

lion *per annum* intereſt.——*America* recovered by the ſword muſt be kept by the ſword, and forts and garriſons muſt be maintained in every province to awe the wretched inhabitants, and to hold them in ſubjection. This will create another addition of expence; and both together cannot, I ſuppoſe, be ſtated at leſs than two millions *per annum*.——But how is ſuch an increaſe of revenue to be procured?——The colonies, deſolated and impoveriſhed, will yield no revenue.—The ſurpluſſes of the ſinking fund have, for many years, formed a neceſſary part of the current and ordinary ſupplies.——It muſt, therefore, be drawn from *new* taxes.——But can the kingdom bear ſuch an increaſe of taxes? Or, if it can, where ſhall we find a ſurplus for diſcharging an enormous debt of above 160 millions? And what will be our condition, when the next foreign war ſhall add two millions *per annum* more to our expences?——Indeed this is a frightful proſpect. But it will be rendered infinitely more frightful by carrying our views to that increaſe of the power of the Crown which will ariſe from the increaſe of the army, from the diſpoſal of new places without number, and the patronage of the whole continent of *North-America*.

Theſe conſequences have been ſtated moderately on the ſuppoſition, that we ſhall ſucceed in ſubduing *America*; and that, while we are doing it,

our

our natural enemies will neglect the opportunity offered them, and continue to satisfy themselves with assisting *America indirectly*.——But should the contrary happen.——I need not say what will follow.

Some time ago this horrid danger might have been avoided, and the colonies kept by the easiest means.——By a prudent lenity and moderation.——By receiving their petitions.——By giving up the right we claim to dispose of their property, and to alter their governments.——By guarantying to them, in these respects, a legislative independence; (*a*) and establishing them in

the

(*a*) " There is something (says a great writer) so unnatural
" in supposing a large society, sufficient for all the good pur-
" poses of an independent political union, remaining subject
" to the direction and government of a distant body of men
" who know not sufficiently the circumstances and exigencies
" of this society; or in supposing this society obliged to be
" governed solely for the benefit of a distant country; that it
" is not easy to imagine there can be any foundation for it
" in justice or equity. The insisting on *old claims* and *tacit*
" *conventions*, to extend civil power over distant nations, and
" form grand unwieldy empires, without regard to the ob-
" vious maxims of humanity, has been one great source of
" human misery." *System of Moral Philosophy*, by Dr. Hutcheson, vol. ii. p. 309. In the section from whence this quotation is taken, Dr. Hutcheson discusses the question,
" When colonies have a right to be released from the domi-
" nion of the parent state?" And his general sentiment seems

to

the poffeffion of equal liberty with ourfelves.——
This a great and magnanimous nation fhould
have done. This, fince the commencement
of hoftilities, would have brought them back
to their former habits of refpect and fubordination; and might have bound them to us for
ever.

MONTESQUIEU has obferved, that ENGLAND, in
planting colonies, fhould have *commerce*, not *dominion*, in view; the increafe of dominion being incompatible with the fecurity of public liberty.—
Every advantage that could arife from commerce
they have offered us without referve; and their
language to us has been——" Reftrict us, as much
" as you pleafe, in *acquiring* property by regu-
" lating our trade for your advantage; but claim
" not the difpofal of that property after it has
" been acquired.—Be fatisfied with the authority
" you exercifed over us before the prefent reign.—
" PLACE US WHERE WE WERE IN 1763."———On
thefe terms they have repeatedly fued for a reconciliation. In return, we have denounced
them *Rebels*; and with our fleets in their ports,

to be, that they acquire fuch a right, " Whenever they are
" fo increafed in numbers and ftrength, as to be fufficient by
" themfelves for all the good ends of a political union."———
Such a decifion given by a wife man, long before we had any
difputes with the colonies, deferves, I think, particular
notice.

and our bayonets at their breasts, have left them no other alternative than to acknowledge our supremacy, and give up rights they think most sacred; or stand on the defensive, and appeal to heaven.—They have chosen the latter.

In this situation, if our feelings for *others* do not make us tremble, our feelings for *ourselves* soon may.——Should we suffer the consequences I have intimated, our pride will be humbled.—— We shall admire the plans of moderation and equity which, without bloodshed or danger, would have kept *America*.——We shall wish for the happiness of former times; and remember, with anguish, the measures which many of us lately offered their lives and fortunes to support.

I must not conclude these observations, without taking particular notice of a charge against the colonies, which has been much insisted on.— " They have, it is said, always had independency " in view; and it is this, chiefly, that has pro- " duced their present resistance."——It is scarcely possible there should be a more unreasonable charge. Without all doubt, our connexion with them might have been preserved for ages to come, (perhaps *for ever*) by wise and liberal treatment. Let any one read a pamphlet published in 1761, by Dr. *Franklin*, and entitled,

The

The interest of Great Britain with respect to her Colonies; and let him deny this if he can.—Before the present quarrel, there prevailed among them the purest affection for this country, and the warmest attachment to the House of HANOVER. And since the present quarrel begun, and not longer ago than the beginning of last winter, independency was generally dreaded among them. There is the fullest evidence for this; and all who are best acquainted with *America*, must know it to be true. As a specimen of this evidence, and of the temper of *America* till the period I have mentioned, I will just recite the following facts.

In the resolutions of the *Assembly*, which met at *Philadelphia*, July 15, 1774, after making the strongest professions of affection to *Britain*, and duty to their sovereign, they declare their abhorrence of every idea of an unconstitutional independence on the parent state.——An assembly of delegates from all the towns of the county of *Suffolk* (of which *Boston* is the capital) delivered in September 1774, to General Gage, a remonstrance against fortifying *Boston-neck*. In this remonstrance, they totally disclaim every wish of independence.——The same is done in the instructions given by the several colonies to the first deputies chosen for a general Congress.——In the petition of the first Congress to the King, they declare

they

they shall always, carefully and zealously, endeavour to support and maintain their connexion with *Great Britain*. In the memorial of the same Congress to the people of this country, they repeat this assurance.——In the order of the *Congress*, which met in May 1775, for a general fast, they call upon all *America* to unite in beseeching the Almighty to avert the judgments with which they were threatened, and *to bless their rightful Sovereign*, that so *a reconciliation might be brought about with the parent state*.——And in their declaration setting forth the causes of their taking arms, they warn us, " that, should they
" find it necessary, foreign assistance was undoubt-
" edly attainable;" but at the same time declare,
" that they did not mean to dissolve the union
" which had so long and so happily subsisted
" between them and this country; that necessity
" had not yet driven them to that desperate
" measure, or induced them to excite any other
" nation to war against us; and that they had
" not raised armies with ambitious designs of
" forming independent states, but solely for the
" protection of their property against violence,
" and the defence of that freedom which was their
" birth-right."——In the instructions, delivered Nov. 9, 1775, by a committee of the representatives of the province of *Pensylvania*, to their delegates in the third general congress; they enjoin

join them, in behalf of the province, " utterly to " reject any propofitions, fhould fuch be made, " that might lead to a feparation from the mother " country."

What reafon can there be for thinking the colonies not fincere in all thefe declarations?—— In truth; it was not poffible they fhould be otherwife than fincere; for fo little did they think of war, at the time when moft of thefe declarations were made, that they were totally unprepared for it: And, even when hoftilities were begun at LEXINGTON in April 1775, they were fo deftitute of every inftrument of defence, particularly ammunition, that *half* the force which is now invading them, would have been fufficient to conquer them at once.

I will beg leave to add on this occafion, the following extracts from letters, written by fome leading perfons at NEW-YORK, the genuinenefs of which may be depended on.

New-York, Auguft 3d. 1775. —— " I am " fenfible of the many artifices and falfhoods " which have been ufed to biafs the minds of " your countrymen, who believe evil reports of " us; and, particularly, that we are aiming at " independence.—— Of this be affured, that even " HANCOCK and ADAMS are averfe to inde- " pendence. There was a lye current laft week, " that the congrefs had finally agreed upon inde-
" pendence

" pendence to take place the 10th of March
" next, should not our grievances be redressed
" before that time. I wrote to one of our
" delegates, to enquire whether this report
" was true. In his answer he declares, upon
" his honour, that he believed there was not
" one man in the Congress who would dare to
" make a motion tending to independence; or,
" that if any one did, two could not be found
" to support the motion.——None but those
" who are on the spot can conceive what a spirit
" is gone forth among all ranks and degrees of
" men.——We deserve to be free. It is a heavy
" sacrifice we are making. Trade is at an end.
" We expect our city to be knocked about our
" ears. But I declare solemnly, I will submit to
" all, and die in a log-house in the wilds of
" America, and be free; rather than flourish in
" servitude."———In a subsequent letter, dated
NEW-YORK, Jan. 3d. 1776, the same person writes
as follows:——" It is in the power of the
" ministry to annihilate all our disputes, by re-
" storing us to the situation we were in at the
" conclusion of the last war. If this is done, we
" shall immediately return to our allegiance.
" But if not, be assured, that an awful scene will
" be opened in the spring. Let me repeat a
" caution to you; believe not the insinuations

" of our enemies, who would make you all believe
" that *independence* is what *America* aims at. It
" is an infidious falfhood. Madmen will be
" found in all large focieties. It would be
" fingular, were there none fuch to be found
" in a body of three millions of people and
" upwards. But they are like a grain of fand on
" the fea fhore."

Another perfon writes thus.——NEW-YORK,
Nov. 2d. 1775. " We love and honour our
" King. He has no fubjects in all his dominions
" more attached to his perfon, family and govern-
" ment, notwithftanding the epithet of rebels be-
" ftowed upon us. No charge is more unjuft
" than the charge that we defire an independence
" on *Great Britain*. Ninety-nine in a hundred
" of the inhabitants of this country deprecate
" this as the heavieft of evils. But if adminiftra-
" tion will perfift in their prefent meafures, this
" will and muft inevitably be the event; for
" fubmit to the prefent claims of the Britifh par-
" liament, while unreprefented in it, you may be
" affured they never will. And what deferves
" notice is, that all the violence of *Britain* only
" unites the *Americans* ftill more firmly together,
" and renders them more determined to be free
" or die. This fpirit is unconquerable by vio-
" lence; but they may be eafily won by kindnefs.

" Serious

"——Serious people of all denominations among us, epifcopal and non-epifcopal, are much employed in prayer to God for the fuccefs of the prefent ftruggles of *America*. They confider their caufe as the caufe of God; and as fuch, they humbly commit it to him, confident of fuccefs in the end, whatever blood or treafure it may coft them."

Since thefe letters were written, the fentiments of *America*, with refpect to *independence*, have been much altered. But it fhould be remembered, that this alteration has been owing entirely to OURSELVES; I mean, to the meafures of the laft winter and fummer, and particularly the following.

Firft. The rejection of the petition from the Congrefs brought over by Governor PENN. In this petition they profeffed, in ftrong language, that they ftill retained their loyalty to the King and attachment to this country; and only prayed, "that they might be directed to fome mode by which the united applications of the Colonies might be improved into a happy reconciliation; and that, in the mean time, fome meafures might be taken for preventing their farther deftruction, and for repealing fuch ftatutes as more immediately diftreffed them."——The Colonies had often petitioned before without being heard. They had, therefore, little hope from this application; and meant that, if rejected, it should be their last.

Secondly. The last prohibitory bill, by which our protection of them was withdrawn; their ships and effects confiscated; and open war declared against them.

Thirdly. Employing *foreign* troops to subdue them. This produced a greater effect in *America* than is commonly imagined. And it is remarkable, that even the writers in *America* who answered the pamphlet entitled COMMON SENSE, acknowledge, that should the *British* ministry have recourse to foreign aid, it might become (*a*) proper to follow their example, and to embrace the necessity of resolving upon *independence*.

I have, further, reason to believe, that the answer to the last petition of the City of London, presented in March 1776, (*b*) had no small share in producing the same effect.

By these measures, and others of the same kind, those Colonists who had all along most dreaded and abhorred independence, were at last reconciled to it.——I can, however, say from

(*a*) See COMMON SENSE, and PLAIN TRUTH, p. 44. Published for Mr. *Almon*.

(*b*) The Colonies, I am assured, were not perfectly unanimous till they saw this answer.

particular

particular information, that even so lately as the month of June laſt, an accommodation might have been obtained with the Colonies, on a reaſonable and moderate plan; without giving up any one of the rights claimed by this country, except that of altering their charters and diſpoſing of their property.——And, as it would have reſtored peace and prevented the deſolating calamities into which *America* and *Britain* are now plunged, no friend to humanity can avoid regretting that ſuch a plan, when offered, was not adopted. But our rulers preferred coercion and conqueſt: And the conſequence has been, that the Colonies, after being goaded and irritated to the utmoſt, reſolved to diſengage themſelves, and directed the CONGRESS to declare them Independent States; which was accordingly done, as is well-known, on the 4th of July laſt. Since that time, they have, probably, been making applications to foreign powers; and it is to be feared, that *now* we may in vain offer them the very terms for which they once ſued.——All this is the neceſſary conſequence of the principles by which human nature is governed.——There was a time when, perhaps, we ſhould ourſelves have acted with more violence; and, inſtead of remonſtrating and praying, as *America* has done, have refuſed the moſt advantageous terms when offered with defiance, and under an awe from a military force.

force. Had King WILLIAM, instead of coming over by invitation to deliver us, invaded us; and, at the head of an army, offered us the BILL OF RIGHTS; we should, perhaps, have spurned at it; and considered LIBERTY itself as no better than SLAVERY, when enjoyed as a boon from an insolent conqueror.——But we have all along acted as if we thought the people of *America* did not possess the feelings and passions of *men*, much less of *Englishmen*.——It is indeed strange our ministers did not long ago see, that they had mistaken the proper method of treating the Colonies; and that though they might be gradually *influenced* to any thing, they could be dragooned to nothing.—Had King *James the Second* avoided violence; and been a little more patient and secret in pursuing his views, he might have gained all he wished for. But an eager haste and an open avowal of the odious claims of prerogative ruined him.——This has been since considered; and a plan both here and in *Ireland*, (a) less *expeditious* indeed, but more *sure*, has been pursued.

(a) I am sorry to differ from those respectable persons who have proposed placing *America* on the same ground with *Ireland*. If the same ground of LAW is meant, it is already done; for our laws give us the same power over *Ireland*, that we claim over *America*. If the same ground of PRACTICE is meant; it has been most unfortunate for *Ireland*, and would be equally so for *America*.

And

And had the same plan been pursued in *America*, the whole empire might in time have been brought, without a struggle, to rest itself quietly in the lap of corruption and slavery. It may, therefore, in the issue prove happy to the Colonies, that they have not been thought worthy of any such cautious treatment. Our coercive measures have done all for them that their warmest patriots could have desired. They have united them among themselves, and bound them together under one government. They have checked them in the career of vicious luxury; guarded them against any farther infection from hence; taught them to seek all their resources within themselves; instructed them in the use of arms; and led them to form a naval and military power which may, perhaps, in time, become superior to any force that can attack them, and prove the means of preserving from invasion and violence, a government of justice and virtue, to which the oppressed in every quarter of the globe may fly, and find peace, protection, and liberty.——In short. These measures have, in all probability, hastened that disruption of the *new* from the *old* world, which will begin a new *æra* in the annals of mankind; (*a*) and produce a revolution more

---

(*a*) See the Abbe RAYNAL's Reflections on this subject at the end of the 18th book of his History of the *European Settlements* in the East and West-Indies.——" Is it not likely,

" says

important, perhaps, than any that has happened in human affairs.——As a friend, therefore, to the general interest of mankind, I ought, probably, to rejoice in these measures; and to bless that all-governing Providence, which, often, out of the evil intended by wretched mortals, brings the greatest good.———But when I consider the *present* sufferings which these measures must occasion, and the *cataſtrophe* with which they threaten GREAT-BRITAIN; I am shocked; and feel myself incapable of looking forward, without distress, to the fate of an empire, once united and happy, but now torn to pieces, and falling a sacrifice to despotic violence and blindness. Under the impression of these sentiments, and dreading the

---

" says this writer, that the distrust and hatred which have of
" late taken place of that regard and attachment which the
" *Engliſh* Colonies felt for the parent country, may hasten their
" separation from one another? Every thing conspires to pro-
" duce this great disruption; the æra of which it is impos-
" sible to know.——Every thing tends to this point: The
" progress of good in the new hemisphere, and the progress
" of evil in the old.——In proportion as our people are
" weakened, and resign themselves to each other's dominion,
" population and agriculture will flourish in *America*; and
" the arts make a rapid progress: And that country rising out
" nothing, will be fired with the ambition of appearing with
" glory in its turn on the face of the globe——O posterity!
" ye, peradventure, will be more happy than your unfortunate
" and contemptible ancestors."——Mr. *Juſtamond*'s Tranſ-
lation.

awful

awful *crisis* before us, I cannot help, however impotent my voice, crying out to this country——
"Make no longer war against *yourselves*. Withdraw your armies from your Colonies. Offer your power to them as a *protecting*, not a *destroying* power. Grant the security they desire to their property and charters; and renounce those notions of dignity, which lead you to prefer the exactions of force to the offerings of gratitude, and to hazard *every thing* to gain *nothing*.——By such wisdom and equity *America* may, perhaps, be still preserved; and that dreadful breach healed, which your enemies are viewing with triumph, and all *Europe* with astonishment."

But what am I doing?——At the moment I am writing this, the possibility of a reconciliation may be lost.——*America* may have formed an alliance with FRANCE——And the die may be cast.

SECT. III.

Of Schemes for raising Money by Public Loans.

THE following observations were occasioned by the scheme for the public loan of last year, proposed to the *House of Commons* at opening the *Budget*, and afterwards agreed to. I have thought

thought proper, therefore, to introduce thefe obfervations here; and, as they appear to me of fome importance, I fhall endeavour to explain them with as much care and perfpicuity as poffible.

In order to raife *two millions*, the Legiflature created laft year a new capital in the 3 *per cent.* confolidated annuities, of 2.150,000l. Every fhare of 77l. 10s. in this new capital was valued at 65l. 17s. 6d. or every 100l. *ftock* at 85l. For the whole new capital, therefore, Government has received in money, 1.827,500l.—The remaining fum, neceffary to make up *two millions*, was a compenfation advanced to Government for relinquifhing the profits of a Lottery, confifting of 60,000 tickets, each of the fame value with 10l. *three per cent. ftock*; and might have been obtained, without annexing the Lottery to the annuities.——This new capital the public may be obliged to redeem at *par*; in which cafe, 322,500l. (being the difference between 1.827,500 and 2.150,000l.) that is $17\frac{1}{2}$ *per cent.* will be paid by the public more than it has received.——In this tranfaction, therefore, Government has acted as a private perfon would act, who, in order to raife 850l. on a mortgage, fhould promife for it 30l. *per ann.* (or $3\frac{1}{2}$ *per cent.* intereft) and 150l. (that is $17\frac{1}{2}$ *per cent.*

nearly) over and above the principal, when the mortgage came to be difcharged.——Such a *premium* (fhould the mortgage be difcharged foon) would be very extravagant; but, if *never* to be difcharged, would be infignificant: Nor would it be poffible to account for fuch a bargain, except by fuppofing, that the borrower, inftead of meaning to repay the fum he borrowed, chofe to continue *always* paying intereft for it, or returning 30l. annually for 850l. once advanced; and to fubject his eftate, for that purpofe, to an eternal incumbrance.

The public, I have faid, may be obliged to difcharge the new capital, lately created, at *par*; and, confequently, to fuffer a lofs by this year's loan of 322,500l. This will, undoubtedly, happen, fhould the nation profper, and the public debts be put into a regular and fixed courfe of redemption; for the 3 *per cents.* would then foon rife to *par*.

The extravagance I have pointed out is the more to be regretted, becaufe it was entirely needlefs; for the fame fum might as well have been borrowed by fchemes, which would not have fubjected the public to the neceffity of paying, when the loan came to be difcharged, more money than had been received.——For inftance. The fum advanced for the new capital of 2.150,000l. *three per cent.* annuities, might have been

been procured by offering 3 ½ *per cent.* on a capital equal to the sum advanced; or on 1.827,500 l. And the remainder, necessary to make up *two millions*, might have been obtained by the profits of a Lottery, consisting of 60,000 tickets each worth 10 l. in MONEY. This scheme would have differed but little in value from the other; and the interest, or the annuity payable by the public, would have been 63,962 l. at 3 ½ *per cent.* on a capital of 1.827,500; (*a*) instead of 64,500 l. at 3 *per cent.* on a capital of 2.150,000 l.

When a 100 l. *stock* in the 3 *per cent.* annuities is sold at 85 ¾, purchasers get 3 ½ *per cent.* interest for their money. When, therefore, the 3 *per cents* are at this price, 3 ½ *per cents* would be at *par*; and a capital of 1.827,500 l. might be redeemed by the public, (without losing any advantage arising from its debts being at a discount,) by paying this sum; or by returning the money borrowed (*b*). But in the same circumstances, a capital

---

(*a*) Had this interest been insufficient, it might have been increased a 16th or even an 8th *per cent.* without any material difference; or, (which would have been better) 3 ½ *per cent.* might have been offered for *four fifths* of the sum borrowed, and 4 *per cent.* for the remainder; in which case, the annuity payable by the public would have been 65,790 l.

(*b*) It should be remembered here, that tho' Government, when its debts are at a discount, may be able, with the consent

capital of 2.150,000l. in the 3 *per cent.* annuities, for which 85l. *per cent.* or, in the whole, 1.827,500l. had been received, could not be redeemed without offering 86 or 87 *per cent.* for it; nor, therefore, without paying *more* than the original sum borrowed.———When the 5 *per cents* are near *par*, there would be a loss of 322,500l. in redeeming the same capital; whereas, the former annuities, for which the same sum had been advanced, might be always discharged by either paying the very sum (*a*) advanced, or a *less sum*.

In

---

sent of the creditors, to redeem a given capital by paying a less sum than that capital; yet it can never be obliged to pay *more*. ———In other words; a 100l. capital in the 3 *per cents*; 3 ½ *per cents*; or 4, or 5 *per cents*, Government is always at liberty to redeem by paying 100l. whatever the market price of it may be, and whether the creditors will consent or not.

(*a*) There is another very great advantage which would attend these annuities.———One and the same *surplus* would discharge a given capital in less time. For example. A surplus of a million *per ann.* invariably applied, and the first payment to be made immediately, would discharge a capital of a *hundred millions* bearing 3 *per cent.* interest in 46 years. But if the same capital bore 3 ½ *per cent.* interest, it would be discharged in 43 ½ years; if 4 *per cent.* in 40 years; if 5 *per cent.* in 37 ¼ years.———A capital *less* than a 100 millions, in the same proportion that the interest is *more* than 3 *per cent.* and for which, therefore, the same annuity is paid, (as in the present case) the same surplus would discharge in 39 years, if the interest is 3 ½; in 34 ¼ years, if the interest is 4 *per cent.*

——In all poffible circumftances, therefore, thefe annuities would have the advantage.——But we never, when contracting debts, carry our views to the difcharge of the principal; and the confequences muft prove fatal.

It

cent. in 27 ½ years if the intereft is 5 *per cent.*——Suppofing, therefore, 75 millions borrowed in the manner of our Government, by creating a capital of a 100 millions bearing 3 *per cent.* (that is, by felling 3 *per cent.* ftock for 75l. in money) which might have been borrowed by creating a capital of only 75 millions bearing 4 *per cent.* (that is by felling 4 *per cent.* ftock at 100) there will not only be a lofs of 25 millions by a needlefs increafe of the capital; but alfo a lofs of 14 millions, by an increafe of the time in which one and the fame faving will difcharge the two capitals.——This may be proved in the following manner.——A million *per ann.* will, in 34 years and a quarter, very nearly difcharge a debt of 75 millions bearing intereft at 4 *per cent*; but the fame faving will, in the fame time, difcharge only a capital of 61 millions, if it bears intereft at 3 *per cent.* When, therefore, fuch a faving has compleated the redemption of the *one* capital, there will remain unpaid of the other, 39 millions. ——What has been now applied to a large fum holds true in proportion of any fmaller fums.

It appears from hence to be a very wrong obfervation which fome have made; "that provided the annual charge is the fame, " it fignifies little what the *principal* of the public debt is." ——As there is no way of removing the annual charge but by paying the *principal*, it is of juft as much confequence what it is, as whether it is practicable or impracticable, to remove a burden which weakens and cripples, and muft in time fink the public. An annuity of SIX MILLIONS, if the principal is

a HUN-

It is necessary I should observe, in justice to our present ministers, that in adopting the scheme on which I have made these remarks, they have only followed the example of former ministers; and that, however needless a waste it occasions of public money, there is reason to fear it will be followed by future ministers; for the increase of difficulty and expence in redeeming the public debts, which such schemes create, being to be felt *hereafter*, it makes no impression, and is little regarded.

In 1759, the fifth year of the last war, the lenders of 6.600,000l. were granted a capital in the 3 *per cents* of 7,590,000l. together with the profits of the Lottery. Subtract from the sum advanced, 150,000l. for the profits of the Lottery; and it will appear, that, in this instance, 1.140,000l. was *needlesly* added to the capital; there being no reason to doubt, but that lenders would then have

---

a HUNDRED MILLIONS borrowed at 6 *per cent.* might be redeemed in 33 years with a million *per ann.* surplus. But if the principal is TWO HUNDRED MILLIONS bearing 3 *per cent.* the same surplus would, in the same time, pay off only 56 millions; and but little more than a *quarter* of the annuity would be redeemed. If, therefore, the same sum might as well have been obtained by creating a principal of a hundred millions bearing 6 *per cent.* as by creating a capital of two hundred millions bearing 3 *per cent.* there will be a needless expence, in discharging the debt, of 144 millions.

readily

readily advanced 6.600,000 l. for a capital of 6.450,000 l. bearing 3 ½ *per cent.* (*a*) intereſt, provided the profits of a Lottery were annexed; inſtead of advancing the ſame ſum for a nominal capital near 18 *per cent.* greater, but bearing 3 *per cent* intereſt.

Again. In 1762, in order to raiſe 12 millions, every contributor of 80 l. was entitled to a capital of 100 l. to bear 4 *per cent.* intereſt for 19 years; and afterwards to become redeemable, and to bear intereſt at 3 *per cent.* And for the remaining 20 l. neceſſary to make up a 100 l. contributors were entitled to an annuity of 1 l. for 98 years.——This was the ſame with promiſing, for every 60 l. advanced, a 100 l. capital in the 3 *per cent.* annuities, not redeemable for 19 years; and, for the remaining 40 l. neceſſary to make up 100 l. an annuity of 2 l. for 19 years; and, after that, of 1 l. for 79 years.

By this ſcheme no leſs a ſum than 4.800,000 l. was needleſsly added to the capital of the public debts. For, had 5 *per cent.* been offered for for every 60 l. advanced; (*b*) and, for the re-
remaining

(*a*) The price of the 3 *per cents* at the time of this loan (in the beginning of Feb. 1759) was 88 ½ and 89.

(*b*) The 3 *per cents* juſt before this loan were at 69 l. and, conſequently, 5 *per cent.* intereſt, (or 3 l. *per ann.* for 60 l.) would

maining 40 l. an annuity of 2 l. during 19 years, and afterwards of 1 l. for 79 years; equal encouragement would have been given to contributors; the annuity payable by the public would have been the fame; and the new capital would have been 7,200,000 l. bearing 5 *per cent.* intereft; which might, at any time, have been redeemed with a faving of a million *per ann.* (the firft payment to be made immediately) in *five* years and a *quarter*: Whereas now, this debt will not become redeemable till 1781; and then, it will form a capital of 12 millions, not capable of being redeemed with the fame faving, in lefs than *nine* years and a half. Five millions and a quarter, (*a*) therefore, will be wafted.

The capital of 12 millions four *per cent.* annuities created this year, were made irredeemable for 19 years, to guard againft the effects of an apprehenfion then unavoidable, that an intereft of 4 *per cent.* would, if the capitals were redeemable, be reduced, whenever peace came, to 3 *per cent.*

would have afforded fubfcribers a profit of 9 l. for every 60 l. advanced. The long annuity was worth, as the ftocks then ftood, 21 years purchafe, and the fhort annuity, 13 years purchafe. Upon the whole loan, therefore, the profit would have been 3 *per cent.*

(*a*) That is, the difference between 12 millions, and the fum bearing intereft at 3 *per cent.* which a million *per ann.* would pay off, in five years and a quarter.

H   as

as had been done in the preceding peace.—But this end would have been anſwered, with equal effect and more advantage to the public, by pledging the faith of Parliament, that whatever intereſt was promiſed on any capital, ſhould not be *reduced* for 19 years; or (which comes to the ſame) that the capital ſhould not be *redeemed*, during that term, by borrowing money, and creating a new capital bearing *lower* intereſt. This would have placed capitals bearing any intereſt on the ſame footing *nearly* with the 3 *per cent.* annuities; and an aſſurance, that no part of them ſhould be diſcharged, without at the ſame time diſcharging an equal capital in the 3 *per cents*, would have placed them *entirely* on the ſame footing.——Had it, however, been neceſſary, on account of the fear of a reduction of intereſt, to make the capital here propoſed bearing 5 *per cent*, and the capitals to be mentioned preſently bearing 4 *per cent.* irredeemable, (and therefore the intereſt irreducible) for any term (ſuppoſe till 1781); had, I ſay, even this been neceſſary (and more could not have been neceſſary) no advantage of great conſequence would have been loſt. Theſe capitals would, during that term, have been exactly the ſame burden on the public with the capitals which were actually created; and after that term, they would have been a much leſs burden, as will be ſhewn at the end of this ſection.

Again.

Again. In January 1760, eight millions were borrowed by offering for this sum a capital of eight millions to carry 4 *per cent.* interest for 21 years, and afterwards 3 *per cent*, together with a *premium* of 240,000 l. stock carrying the same interest, and divided into 80,000 l. lottery tickets, each 3 l. stock.——This was the same with offering, for 80 l. of every 100 l. advanced, a capital of 100 l. in the 3 *per cent.* annuities, (*a*) not redeemable for 21 years; and for the remainder besides a lottery ticket an annuity of 1 l. for 21 years.——The same sum might have been raised by offering 4 *per cent*, irreducible during 21 years, or 3 l. *per ann.* for 75 l. of every 100 l. advanced, and for the remaining 25 l. an annuity of 1 l. for 21 years, together with a lottery ticket.——In this case, the new capital, instead of 8.240,000 l. bearing 3 *per cent.* not subject to redemption, and having an annuity of 82,400 l. annexed to it, for 21 years; would have been 6.000,000 l. bearing 4 *per cent.* with

(*a*) The 3 *per cents* being at this time at 80 l. an annuity of 3 l. purchased for 75 l. would have produced a profit of 5 l. Therefore these schemes are of exactly the same value. But they are too narrow; and the subscription this year fell immediately to one *per cent.* discount. But in the scheme I have proposed this might have been prevented by only offering 4 *per cent.* for 77 l. or 78 l. (instead of 75 l.) of every 100 l.

the same annuity annexed, but redeemable at *any* time; and 2;0,000*l.* (*a*) bearing 4 *per cent.* for 21 years, and afterwards 3 *per cent.*

By the scheme likewise in 1761, for borrowing 11.400,000*l.* a capital of 100*l.* bearing 3 *per cent. interest*, was given for part of every 100*l.* advanced; and for the other part, an annuity of 1*l.* 2*s.* 6*d.* for 99 years. Had, in this case, 75*l.* FOUR *per cent.* STOCK, been offered for 75*l.* in *money*; and, for the remaining 25*l.* necessary to make up 100*l.* the said annuity of 1*l.* 2*s.* 6*d.* for 99 years; (*b*) the whole annual charge would have been the same; subscribers could not have been sensible of any difference in the encouragement offered them; and the public, in paying its debts, would have saved 2.850,000*l.*

There was also this year 600,000*l.* received by government for 600,000*l.* stock, carrying 3 *per cent.* interest, and divided into 60,000 lottery tickets, each worth 10*l.* in stock.—As 150,000*l.* of this sum was paid for the profits of the lottery;

(*a*) It is plain, that this capital, as well as the former, might have been a quarter (or 60,000*l.*) less, which would have made the whole saving of capital 2.060,000*l.*

(*b*) At the time of this loan, the 3 *per cents.* were above 75; and, therefore, a perpetual annuity of 3*l.* could not be purchased for 75*l.* and an annuity of 1*l.* 2*s.* 6*d.* for 99 years, was worth at least 27*l.* This, therefore, would have been a scheme very profitable to subscribers.

and

and as 4 *per cent.* could not at this time be made of money laid out in the funds, it is out of doubt, that the same sum (or 600,000*l.*) would have been given for 450,000*l.* stock, carrying 4 *per cent.* and divided into 60,000 lottery tickets, each of the same value with 7*l.* 10*s.* four *per cent.* stock; and thus 150,000*l.* more would have been saved.

In like manner; it will appear, that *three millions*, raised in 1757, by creating a capital of *three millions* bearing 3 *per cent.* interest, (*a*) with a life annuity annexed of 1*l.* 2*s.* 6*d.* for every 100*l.* advanced; and also, *four millions and a half* raised in 1758, by creating a capital of *four millions and a half*, bearing 3 *per cent.* with an annuity of a *half per cent.* annexed for 24 years; might have been

(*a*) The life-annuity granted in this case could not have been worth so little as 16*l.* or 14 years purchase; and, therefore, a capital of 100*l.* in the 3 *per cents* was sold for 84*l*; or a capital of three millions, for 2.520,000*l.*——A premium, therefore, was granted of 480,000*l*; and this was done without the least reason. For the 3 *per cents* being at that time at 87 and 88, 2.520,000*l.* would undoubtedly have been lent at 3½ *per cent.* interest; and the remaining 480,000*l.* necessary to make up three millions, would have been given for the life annuities; in which case, the annual charge occasioned by the new capital would have been somewhat less; and 480,000*l.* would have been saved, together with the additional expence occasioned by the longer time which a given surplus would require to discharge a debt bearing 3 *per cent.* interest, as explained in the note, p. 94.

raised by creating, in the former case, a capital of two millions and a half, and, in the latter, a capital of four millions, bearing $3\frac{1}{2}$ per cent. interest, with the same annuities annexed.

In 1758, the additional sum of half a million was borrowed at 3 per cent. by a lottery, consisting of 50,000 tickets, each of the same real value with 10*l.* stock, but sold to the subscribers for 10*l.* in money (*a*). As the 3 per cents. were now at 94,

$3\frac{1}{4}$ per

(*a*) It is a general and certain maxim " that whenever " money is borrowed by a lottery which gives a right " to stock equal to the sum advanced, there is a loss " equal to the sum which might have been received for " the profits of the lottery." ——When the 3 per cents. are at 76 or 77, half a million might be borrowed by a lottery, consisting of 50,000 tickets, each of the same value with 10*l.* three per cent. stock: and hitherto such a method of borrowing has been reckoned advantageous. But it only gives a fallacious appearance of borrowing at 3 per cent. It is the same with selling the profits of a lottery, and at the same time absurdly converting the purchase-money into a debt due to the purchaser.——Since the last war we have had seven of these lotteries, including two in 1763; and above a million has been lost by them.

In Queen *Anne*'s time, there were several lotteries, consisting of all *prizes* and no *blanks*. This is so curious, and most persons may be so much at a loss to conceive of the possibility of it, that I cannot help explaining it.

A capital, equal to the whole money advanced, was distributed *equally* among all the tickets in the lottery; and, in order to make them prizes of different values, there was farther distributed among them different shares of an additional

capital,

$3\frac{1}{2}$ *per cent.* could not be made of money laid out in the funds. Therefore, 350,000*l.* of this half capital, to which a right was given, though no money had been paid for it.——For example——In 1711, two millions were raised by a lottery of this kind, called a clafs lottery. The whole fum advanced was divided into 20,000 tickets, each 100*l.* ftock bearing 6 *per cent.* interest. This capital was increafed by a gratuitous capital of 602,200*l.* bearing the fame interest, and divided into fhares which were added to the tickets, in order to form prizes.——This was the fame with giving near 8 *per cent.* for money, befides a *premium* of 30 *per cent.*——As the interest of money was at this time 6 *per cent.* the fum borrowed would most certainly have been advanced at 8 *per cent.* without any *premium*; but it was, I fuppofe, reckoned neceffary that government fhould not *feem* to give fuch high interest.——In the fame year, 1.500,000*l.* was borrowed by another fuch lottery, and creating a capital of 1.928,570*l.* And in 1712, 3.600,000*l.* was borrowed by two more fuch lotteries, and creating a capital of 4.683,080*l.*——The greateft part of the debts contracted by thefe lotteries (amounting to 9.213,850*l.* though only 7.100,000*l.* was advanced) remains at this hour an incumbrance on the public; and the duties conftituting the *general fund* are charged with the interest of it.

In 1714, the national interest was reduced to 5 *per cent.* But in that very year 1.400,000*l.* was borrowed by a lottery, which gave a right to a capital of 1.876,000*l.* bearing 4 *per cent.* that is, by giving near $5\frac{1}{2}$ *per cent.* interest, befides a *premium* of 34 *per cent.*——Thus have our debts been increafed. But even worfe has been done. The taxes charged with the interest of the public debts proving often deficient, the fhorteft way of difcharging the arrears has been often taken, by adding them to the principal, and paying *compound* interest for money.——Is it a wonder, that a nation which has been fo carelefs in contracting debts, fhould have done fo little towards difcharging them?

million might have been raised at $3\frac{1}{2}$ per cent. interest, and the remaining 150,000 l. might have been procured for the profits of the lottery. Or (which is the same) 10 l. each would have been given for 50,000 tickets, of the same value taken all together, with 350,000 l. carrying $3\frac{1}{2}$ per cent. interest; and a capital of 150,000 l. would have been saved.

The same is true of the lottery, by which half a million was borrowed in 1756.——A million and a half also borrowed in this year, by creating a capital of a million and a half, bearing $3\frac{1}{2}$ per cent. for 15 years, and afterwards 3 per cent. might have been procured, by creating a capital of only 1.400,000 l. bearing $3\frac{1}{4}$ per cent. interest. But I will not examine any more of these loans, Let us next consider how detrimental they have been to the public.

All the savings and surplus monies of the kingdom from 1763 to 1775, have amounted (deducting 400,000 l. gained by debts discharged at a discount) to 10.739,793 l. and with this sum 11.139,793 l. of the national debt has been paid off. (See the *Postscript* at the end of this work.) ——The needless addition which was made to the capital of the national debt, by injudicious schemes for raising money during the last war, exceeded this sum; and it follows, therefore, that the whole surplus of the revenue for twelve years, has

has not been sufficient to discharge the capital, to which in the last war a right was given, without receiving any money for it, or obtaining the least advantage by it.

The attentive reader must have observed, as I have gone along, that the extravagance on which I have insisted, has been the consequence of not separating, in the schemes for raising money, the premiums (consisting of short and long and life-annuities) from the perpetual annuities, and requiring them to be distinctly paid for; and also, of not attending to the difference between selling an *annuity*, and selling the *stock* for which that annuity is paid. When a 100*l. stock* in the 3 *per cents.* is at any given price, there is no one who would not be glad to purchase from government a perpetual annuity of 3*l*. at any *lower* price (*a*). But when government sells the *stock*, instead of the *annuity*, at that price, the public is injured in the manner I have represented.

Would any one, in selling any part of his property, offer to make the purchase-money an outstanding principal which he shall be bound to

---

(*a*) That is, in other words; there is no one who would not be glad to lend to government on any higher interest than that which he can make in the funds. There is no one, for instance, who would not be glad to lend 75*l*. at 4 *per cent*. when the 3 *per cents.* are at 76, and when, therefore, he cannot make 4 *per cent*. by purchasing them.

return?

return? (*a*) This is what government has uniformly done in its propofals for raifing money.—Were I to defire any fum to be lent me *without* intereft, offering as a *compenfation* or *premium* an annuity for a given term, or an advantageous contract; the propofal would not be accepted, unlefs the annuity or the contract was worth the fum to be lent; and I fhould make myfelf a debtor to the purchafer for the very thing which I fold to him. ——The abfurdity would be the fame, if inftead of borrowing *without* intereft, I fhould in the fame way borrow at a *low* inteteft. In every fuch bargain, I fhould bring upon myfelf a needlefs debt, equal to the value of the *premium*.

I am afraid I have tired my reader's attention on this fubject. But as much depends upon a right underftanding of it, I am anxious about fhewing it in every poffible light. In hopes, therefore, of being attended to a little longer, I fhall endeavour to give a yet fuller view of this fubject, and to prove its importance, by recapitulating fome of the foregoing remarks, and comparing the *prefent* ftate of our public debts, with

(*a*) The expectation of receiving back fome time or other the purchafe-money would probably, in private loans, influence a purchafer. But in the cafes to which I allude, this certainly was not confidered, and did not at all influence. And if it had influenced, the obfervations I have made as I have gone along, demonftrate that the fame loans would have been made without any fuch expectation.

that which would have been their ſtate, had the errors I have pointed out, in the ſchemes of the public loans during the laſt war, been avoided.

The ſum of 12 millions, borrowed in 1762, would have left, at the end of the war, a redeemable capital of 7.200,000l. carrying 5 *per cent.* intereſt, with an annuity added of 120,000l. for 18 years from January 1763, inſtead of an *ir*-redeemable capital of 12 millions carrying 4 *per cent.* for 18 years, and afterwards 3 *per cent.* See page 95, &c.

The ſum of 12 millions, borrowed in 1761, would have left a redeemable capital of 9 millions bearing 4 *per cent.* intereſt, with a long annuity annexed; inſtead of 12 millions with the ſame annuity annexed. Page 100.

The ſum of 8 millions, borrowed in 1760, would have left a redeemable capital of 6.180,000l. carrying 4 *per cent.* with an annuity of 82,400l. for 18 years from January 1763; inſtead of 8.240,000l. *ir*-redeemable, and carrying 4 *per cent.* for 18 years, and afterwards 3 *per cent.* Page 99.

The ſum of 6.600,000l. borrowed in 1759, would have left a capital of 6.450,000l. carrying 3 $\frac{1}{2}$ *per cent*; inſtead of a capital of 7.590,000l. carrying 3 *per cent.* Page 95.

The ſum of five millions, borrowed in 1758, would have left a redeemable capital of 4.350,000l. bearing 3 $\frac{1}{2}$ *per cent.* intereſt, with an annuity

added

added of 22,500 l. for 19 years from Midsummer 1763; instead of a capital of five millions irredeemable, and carrying 3 ½ *per cent.* for 19 years, and afterwards 3 *per cent.* Page 101, 102, &c.

The sum of three millions, borrowed in 1757, would have left a capital of two millions and a half bearing 3 ½ *per cent.* interest, instead of three millions bearing 3 *per cent.* interest.——And two millions, borrowed in 1756, instead of leaving a capital of two millions, would have left a capital of only 1.750,000 l. Page 104.

The result, therefore, is, that the whole capital of the public debts would have been, at the end of the last war, near TWELVE MILLIONS AND A HALF less than it was; and at the same time, the annual charge not greater.——In 1775, the difference would have been much more considerable. For,

Supposing all the same sums applied since the last war to the discharge of the public debts that we know have been so applied, not only the *capital* but the *annual charge* would have been considerably less.——This will be demonstrated by the following account.

It may be learnt from the *Postscript* at the end of this Tract, that 11.139,793 l. of the public debts has been discharged with 10.739,793 l. of the public money, derived from various savings and surplusses. All this money *might* have been employed,

employed, and without doubt *would* have been employed, in redeeming first the capital I have mentioned in Page 107, of 7.200,000 l. bearing 5 *per cent.* interest; and afterwards, the two other capitals there mentioned of 9 millions, and of 6,180,000l. bearing 4 *per cent.* interest. It would have been sufficient to redeem the whole of the former capital, and also 3.539,793 l. of the two last capitals; which would have set free for the public an annual charge of 501,591 l.——To this sum must be added an annual charge of 256,000l. saved in 1765, 1766, 1767 and 1768, by redeeming, with 6.400,000l. borrowed in those years, so much of a debt unfunded at the end of the war, but afterwards funded, and carrying 4 *per cent.* interest. And also 12,537 l. *per ann.* gained by changing 1.253,700 l. from an interest of 4 to 3 *per cent.* and 7,500 l. *per ann.* gained in 1771, by the ceasing of an annuity of a $\frac{1}{2}$ *per cent.* annexed for 15 years to 1.500,000 l. borrowed in 1756.——The total decrease, therefore, of the annual charge would have been 777,628 l.——But at the same time there would have been the following additions to it.——First. There would have been the addition of 199,500 l. *per ann.* being the interest of 6.650,000 l. borrowed since 1763.——Secondly. Of 69,187 l. *per ann.* being the interest of 2.306,240l. applied, in 1764 and 1765, to the discharge

charge of German and army debts derived from the war, and which might have been converted into a funded capital bearing 3 *per cent.* intereft, by borrowing money to pay them off, in order to avoid diverting money employed in redeeming capitals bearing 5 *per cent.*

Thefe two fums make 268,687 l. which deducted from 777,628 l. leaves 508,941 l. And this is the clear annual charge which would have been faved to the public, exclufive of the favings which have arifen from the falling in of life-annuities.

But the annual charge that has in fact been faved is only 382,129 (*a*).——The difference is 126,812 l.——With this additional faving, as it fell in and increafed from time to time during the courfe of 12 years, a million more of the public debts bearing 4 *per cent.* might have been redeemed; and this would have made a farther faving of 40,000 l. *per ann.* It appears, therefore, upon the whole, that had the miftakes I have pointed out, in the loans of the laft war, been avoided, (all other public meafures remaining the fame) the nation would *now* have had 13 millions and a half lefs to pay, in order to redeem its debts; and alfo an annual charge upon it 166,812 l. lefs.

(*a*) See the Poftfcript.

All this fuppofes that the capitals of the 5 *per cent.* and 4 *per cent.* annuities in the improved fchemes were redeemable.—But had they been made irredeemable till 1781, as mentioned in page 98, the public would not have been much lefs benefited: For, foon after 1781, thefe 5 and 4 *per cents.* (the former 7.200,000 l. and the latter 15.180,000 l.) might have been eafily reduced to 3 ½ *per cent.* and this would have occafioned an annual faving of 183,900 l. over and above the favings, which would have arifen in that year, from the extinction of the fhort annuities.

I will add, that had thefe annuities been made not only *irredeemable* till 1781; but *irreducible* for fome time beyond that year, in the manner intimated in page 98, the public would ftill have been greatly benefited. For, the annual charge upon it would not at any time have been greater; but its debts would have been 12 millions and a half lefs; and, at the fame time, they would have been capable of being difcharged with more expedition, and at a lefs expence, than a fmaller quantity of its prefent debts. See the note, page 94.

I cannot doubt but that all who will attentively examine thefe obfervations will find them to be juft.——I have confined my enquiries to the loans of the laft war. Had I extended them to all our loans, it would have appeared, that a greater fum than

than moſt perſons can think credible, (*a*) has been ſuch a needleſs addition to our debts as I have explained; or, " a pure and uncompenſated loſs, " which might have been avoided by only framing " differently the ſchemes of the public loans."

(*a*) Sixteen Millions have been ſpecified. It will come in my way to mention above Four Millions more in the ſecond ſection of the next part. Notes 1, 12, 14.—No notice has been here taken of the loans of the war before the laſt; but loſſes of the ſame kind to a great amount were incurred by them.

[113]

PART III.

SECT. I.

ABSTRACT of the EXPORTS from and IMPORTS to GREAT-BRITAIN from 1697 to 1773, with REMARKS.

	IMPORTS. £.	EXPORTS. £.	EXCESS of EXPORTS. £.	
ANNUAL MEDIUM for FOUR Years ended at 1700	4,956,975	6,034,724	1,077,749	or $\frac{10}{50}$ of the exports.
For FIVE Years ended at 1710	5,321,717	6,713,246	1,391,529	or $\frac{10}{48}$ of the exports.
at 1715	5,304,343	7,401,946	2,097,603	or $\frac{10}{35}$ of the exports.
at 1725	6,628,279	9,663,527	3,035,248	or $\frac{10}{32}$ of the exports.
at 1735	7,470,454	11,855,226	4,384,772	or $\frac{10}{27}$ of the exports.
at 1745	7,363,079	11,922,982	4,559,903	or $\frac{10}{25}$ of the exports.
at 1750	7,429,739	12,877,129	5,447,390	or $\frac{10}{24}$ of the exports.
at 1755	8,264,834	13,406,530	5,141,696	or $\frac{10}{26}$ of the exports.
at 1760	8,877,144	14,253,377	5,376,233	or $\frac{10}{26}$ of the exports.
For FOUR Years ended at 1764	10,110,870	15,793,158	5,682,228	or $\frac{10}{28}$ of the exports.
For NINE Years ended at 1773	11,996,769	14,814,074	2,817,305	or $\frac{10}{53}$ of the exports.

This ABSTRACT has been formed from the accounts delivered annually to the HOUSE OF COMMONS, and lately publifhed by Sir CHARLES WHITWORTH.

In order to draw juft inferences from it, the following particulars fhould be remembered.—— Firft. The EXPORTS in the *Cuftom-Houfe* entries are, for reafons well-known, too high. This excefs has, by fome of the beft judges, been reckoned at a million *per ann.*——Secondly. The IMPORTS are too low, no fmuggled commodities being included in them. This deficiency has been eftimated at another million *per ann.* But, in order to be fure of keeping within bounds, I will take both at a *million and a half per ann.*——Thirdly. The intereft of the national debt paid to foreigners; the money fpent in foreign countries by *Englifh* travellers; the bullion confumed in manufactures; and the wear of the current coin, cannot, perhaps, amount to much lefs than two millions *per ann.* I will, however, take them at no more than the annual fum which has been commonly fuppofed to be due to foreigners from our funds; or, a *million and a half.*——In order, therefore, to find the GRAND BALANCE OF PAYMENT between *Britain* and the reft of the world *fince* the laft war, all thefe fums (making up THREE MILLIONS) muft be deducted from the excefs of the exports. ——But, in order to find the fame balance *before*

the

the end of the laſt war, leſs muſt be deducted, in proportion as the national debt and the foreign trade were *then* leſs than they are *now*.

If the foregoing Abſtract is examined with a due regard to this rule, it will be found that, from (*a*) 1710 to 1764, the BALANCE OF PAYMENT muſt have been in favour of *Britain*; and that conſequently, there muſt have been, during that period, an influx of money into the kingdom.— It was this, together with the increaſe of our paper, that produced the rapid fall of intereſt which began a few years before the *Acceſſion*. And it was this alſo that enabled us to bear the great expence of the two laſt wars, and the loſs of thoſe enormous ſums which were ſent out of the kingdom to pay foreign ſubſidies, and to ſupport armies on the continent.

Before 1710 it appears to be doubtful, whether the exceſs of the exports was ſuch as brought any money into the kingdom; but it ſeems certain, that it could not have been ſuch as in any degree compenſated that drain of the public caſh, which was occaſioned by the continental wars of King

(*a*) In the exports, as delivered to the *Houſe of Commons*, is included bullion exported. If this, as well as the other ſums I have mentioned, is deducted, there will be ſtill a balance left in favour of *Britain* during this period. Since 1764, it does not appear, from the accounts laid before the *Houſe of Commons*, as publiſhed by Sir *Charles Whitworth*, that any bullion has been entered for exportation.

William and Queen *Ann*. In confequence of this, the quantity of *fpecie* in the kingdom muſt have been greatly diminiſhed; and Dr. *Davenant* computes that in 1711 it was nine millions lefs than at the *Revolution*. Hence proceeded the high rate of intereſt; the unproductivenefs of the taxes; and the difficulties which government met with in raifing money during thofe two wars: And there is reafon to believe, thefe difficulties would have been infurmountable, had not a fubſtitute for *fpecie* been provided by the eſtabliſhment of the *Bank*.

In the interval of peace between the two laſt wars, or from 1748 to 1755, the balance in favour of *Britain* was at the higheſt; and this contributed to raife the ſtocks (*a*) to fuch a price, as enabled government to reduce the intereſt of the public debts from 4 to 3 *per cent*.

But the obfervation I here intended principally to make is, that the *balance*, fince the year 1764, appears, from the preceding abſtract, to have been *againſt* BRITAIN; and that this accounts for the high price of bullion, the fcarcity of fpecie, and the diſtreſs of the *Bank* from that year to 1773.

(*a*) The 3 *per cent*. annuities were then at 105; and, during the firſt five years of the war which began in 1755, they were higher than they have generally been *fince* the war.

It deserves farther to be observed that, while the exports were decreasing from 1764 to 1773, the IMPORTS appear to have increased faster than ever: And the fact is, that since 1760, a greater addition has been made to them, than had been made during the whole time from the *Accession* to that year.———This is a striking proof that luxury has been for some years increasing with rapidity among us; and it is worth adding, that the productiveness of the taxes has kept pace, as might have been expected, with this increase of luxury, both the CUSTOMS and EXCISES having brought in lately, near 250,000l. *per ann.* each, more than they did twelve years ago.———It should be attended to, that this improvement of the revenue must be the effect solely of an increased consumption occasioned by luxury; the taxes, ever since the end of the last war, having been nearly the same.

The *exports* from 1710 to 1764 went on increasing constantly. I have observed, that from 1764 to 1773 they have decreased. One reason of this has been, the decline of the PORTUGAL trade; the exports to that country having fallen, since 1760, from 1.200,000l. *per ann.* to 600,000l. *per ann.*———Another reason has been the check which a wretched policy has been giving, ever since 1763, to our trade with the Colonies. This trade had for many years contributed more than any other

other trade towards raifing our *exports*; and even in the period between 1763 and 1774, notwithftanding the checks it received, it went on increafing, and produced a balance in our favour of a million and a half *per ann.* But fince 1774 it has been entirely loft. *Before* this lofs, the balance of payment between us and the reft of the world was, according to the account I have given, *againft* us. Undoubtedly then, it was a lofs we could by no means have fuftained, had it not been for the feafonable interpofition of fome very particular caufes. Time will fhew whether thefe caufes are of a permanent nature, or temporary and accidental.

SECT. II.

HISTORICAL DEDUCTION and ANALYSIS of the PUBLIC DEBTS.

STATE and AMOUNT of the NATIONAL DEBT, at Midsummer, 1775, with the Charges of Management.

CAPITALS and ANNUITIES transferrable at the BANK OF ENGLAND.

	Principal. £.	Interest. £.
CAPITAL of their original Fund—See Note (1) p. 125 — —	3,200,000	96,000
EXCHEQUER bills, by 3d of *Geo.* I. c. 8th, bearing originally 5 *per cent.* interest, but reduced to 4 *per cent.* in 1727, and to 3 *per cent.* by 23d *George* II. 1749. See Note (2) p. 126 -	500,000	15,000
Purchased of the SOUTH SEA COMPANY in 1722,—reduced from 6 to 5 *per cent.* interest in 1717; from 5 to 4 *per cent.* in 1727; and to 3 *per cent.* by 23d of *George* II. 1749.—See Note (3) — —	4,000,000	120,000
Carried over	7,700,000	231,000
		Lent

	Principal. £.	Interest. £.
Brought over —	7,700,000	231,000
Lent to government at 4 *per cent.* in 1728, charged on the surplus of the fund for the lottery in 1714, and reduced to 3 *per cent.* by 23d *George* II. 1749	1,250,000	37,500
Lent at 4 *per cent.* in 1727; charged on the duties on coals; and reduced to 3 *per cent.* by 23d of *George* II. 1749 — —	1,750,000	52,500
Lent at 4 *per cent.* in 1746; charged on licences for retailing spirituous liquors; and reduced to 3 *per cent.* by 23d *Geo.* II. 1749 —	986,800	29,604
Amount of Bank capital £.	11,686,800	350,604

See Note (4) p. 126.
Charge of management 5,898*l. per ann.*

BANK ANNUITIES.

Consolidated 4 *per cent.* annuities due *April* 5, and *October* 10 — See Note (5) — —	18,986,300	759,452
Carried over £	30,673,100	1,110,056

These annuities fall to 3 *per cent.* in *January*, 1781.
Charge of management 10,680*l. per ann.*

Annuities

	Principal.	Interest.
Brought over —£.	30.673,100	1.110,056
Annuities at 3½ per cent. 1758, due *Jan.* 5, and *July* 5.—These annuities fall to 3 per cent. in 1782 — — See an account of them in p. 101. Charge of management 2,805 *l. per ann.* including management on half a million raised at the same time by a lottery, and made a part of the consolidated 3 per cents.	4.500,000	157,500
CONSOLIDATED 3 per cent. annuities due *Jan.* 5, and *July* 5. See Note (6) Management 21,087 *l. per ann.*	38.251,696	1.147,551
REDUCED 3 per cent. annuities, due *April* 5, and *Oct.* 10. See Note (7) Charge of management 10,324 *l. per ann.*	18.353,774	550,613
Three *per cent.* 1726, due *Jan.* 5, and *July* 5, charged on the deduction of 6 *d. per* pound on all pensions from the civil list; and on all payments from the crown, except to the navy and army—See Note (8) p. 128 —	1.000,000	30,000
Carried over £.	92.778,560	2.995,720
Management 360 *l. per ann.*		Long

	Principal. £.	Interest. £.
Brought over —	92.778,560	2.995,720
Long annuity due *Jan.* 5, and *July* 5 — —	6.702,750	248,250
The remaining term from *Jan.* 1776, is 84 years— See Note (9) p. 128.		
Management 3,491 *l. per ann.*		
CAPITALS and ANNUITIES transferrable at the SOUTH SEA HOUSE.		
SOUTH SEA STOCK —	3.662,784	109,884
The dividend on this stock, at 3¼ *per cent.* is 128,197*l.* 9*s.*—Due *Jan.* 5, and *July* 5.		
SOUTH SEA 3 *per cent.* OLD Annuities due *April* 5, and *Oct.* 10	11.907,470	357,224
Three *per cent.* NEW Annuities due *Jan.* 5, and *July* 5 — —	8.494,830	254,845
Three *per cent.* 1751, due *Jan.* 5, and *July* 5 —	1.919,600	57,588
Charge of management on *South Sea* Stock and Annuities 15,100 *l. per ann.*—See Note (10).		
Carried over £.	125.465,994	4.023,511

CAPITAL

	Principal. £.	Interest. £.
Brought over —	125.465,994	4.023,511
CAPITAL and ANNUITIES transferrable at the INDIA HOUSE.		
EAST INDIA STOCK — Interest 3 per cent. Dividend 7 per cent. 224,000l. due *Jan.* 5, and *July* 5.———— See Note (11). Charge of management 1.285l. 14s. 4d.	3.200,000	96,000
EAST INDIA Annuity due *April* 5, and *Oct.* 10, charged on the surplus of a tax on spirituous liquors. See Note (12) Management 401l. 15s. 8d. per ann.	1.000,000	30,000
ANNUITIES payable at the EXCHEQUER.		
ANNUITIES for 96 and 99 years, from various dates, in the time of King *William* and Queen *Anne*—See Note (13) — — Salaries to Exchequer officers, and management—5,250l. per ann. Annuities for lives, with benefit of survivorship, granted by the 4th of	1.836,276	131,203
Carried over £.	131.502,270	4.280,714

William

	Principal. £.	Interest. £
Brought over —	131.502,270	4.280,714
William and *Mary*, 1693.— Thefe annuities are not yet extinct, and they are valued at three years purchafe	22,781	7,567
Annuities for lives, with benefit of furvivorfhip, by an Act of the 5th of *Geo.* III. 1765—See Note (14) — —	18,000	540
Annuities for two or three lives, granted in 1694.— Alfo, Annuities on fingle lives 1745, 1746, and 1757. —See Note (15)—— Their original amount, taken all together, was very nearly 124,000*l.* but they are now reduced by deaths to near 80,000*l.* and their value is here taken at 10 years purchafe —	800,000	80,000
UNFUNDED DEBT, confifting of Exchequer bills, (1.250,000*l.*) Navy debt, (1.850,000*l.*) and Civil lift debt, fuppofed 500,000*l.*—The intereft is reckoned at 2 *per cent.*—See Note (16)	3.600,000	72,000
Salaries to Exchequer bill officers 650*l. per ann.*		
Total of the principal and intereft of the National Debt at *Midfummer* 1775.	£. 135.943,051	4.440,821

NOTES *containing an* EXPLANATION *and* HISTORY *of the different Articles in the foregoing Account.*

NOTE (1).——BANK OLD CAPITAL. See Page 119.——The BANK was established in 1694. Their original capital was 1.200,000*l.* bearing 8 *per cent.* interest, charged on ⅜ths. of 9*d.* *per* barrel excise, with 4000*l. per ann.* for management.——In 1709, they lent to government 400,000*l.* without interest, which increased their old capital to 1.600,000*l.* bearing 6 *per cent.* interest. In 1742, they again lent to government 1.600,000*l.* without interest; and thereby increased this capital to its present amount, or to 3.200,000*l.* bearing 3 *per cent.* with the same annual sum for management.——It is of particular importance to observe with respect to the sums of 400,000*l.* and of 1.600,000*l.* just mentioned, that they were properly a compensation from the *Bank* to the public for continuing their exclusive privileges; and would have been advanced, or at least the greatest part of them, though government had not bound itself to return the purchase money, by making it a part of the principal due to the *Bank,* provided the same interest had been continued for some time on their former principal, and the same liberty granted to increase their *stock.*——The like is true of 1.200,000*l.* advanced by the *India* Company without interest in 1708.—In these instances, therefore, a needless addition was made to the public debt of 3.200,000*l.* which, had it been avoided, the public would have had not only a principal so much less to pay; but it would have saved in interest at least 96000*l. per ann.* for the old capital of the *Bank* and the capital of the *East India* Company would have formed, in this case, between them, a debt of only 3.200,000*l.* (instead of 6.400,000*l.*) the interest of which might long ago have been reduced at least one half; or from 8 *per cent.* the original interest, to 4 *per cent.*

NOTE (2)——*Half a million*, part of the BANK CAPITAL. See Page 119.——This part of the Bank capital confisted originally of two millions in *Exchequer* bills, cancelled for government by an act of the 3d of *Geo*. I. But half a million was difcharged in 1729; and a million in 1738.

NOTE (3)——FOUR MILLIONS purchafed of the SOUTH-SEA COMPANY; part of the BANK Capital. See Page 119.——In order to procure this money, the *Bank* fold new ftock at 18 *per cent.* premium. This produced a faving of 610,169*l.* the fale of 3.389,831 *l. ftock* having produced four millions in *money*. And, confequently, though by this tranfaction the capital for which they received interest was increafed four millions, yet the *ftock* on which they made their dividends was increafed only 3.389,831*l.*

NOTE (4)——BANK STOCK and DIVIDEND.——The *ftock* on which the *Bank* divides is only 10,780,000*l.* This dividend varies as their profits vary; but for feveral years it has been $5\frac{1}{2}$ *per cent.* payable half-yearly at *Lady-day* and *Michaelmas*. Their whole annual dividend is, therefore, 592,900*l.* which fubtracted from 350,604*l.* the intereft paid by government, makes their clear annual profit 242,296*l.*——Befides intereft, they receive for management of their capital 4000*l. per ann.* on account of their old capital, and 1,898*l. per ann.* on account of four millions purchafed of the South Sea Company; in all, 5,898*l. per ann.*——The *Bank* receives farther the fums fpecified in the foregoing account, towards bearing the expences of managing the annuities commonly called *Bank Annuities*. All thefe expences, including the fums granted for managing their capital, amount to 54,645*l. per ann.*

NOTE (5)——CONSOLIDATED 4 *per cent.* BANK ANNUITIES. See Page 120.——The capital of thefe Annuities confifts of two loans, one in 1760, and the other in 1762, confolidated

folidated into one ſtock, and charged on the additional duty of 3 *d*. per buſhel on malt, the ſurplus of the duties on ſpirituous liquors, and the additional duties on windows; all which duties were ordered by 2d Geo. III. to be carried to the Sinking Fund, and the intereſt with which they were charged to be paid out of that fund.——I have made ſome remarks on theſe loans in page 96, and page 99. They amounted to 20.240,000*l*. But 1.253,700*l*. of this capital was changed in 1770, from an intereſt of 4 to 3 *per cent*. and the capital reduced to the preſent ſum.——A more full account of theſe annuities may be found in Mr. *Aſhmore's* Analyſis of the ſeveral Bank Annuities, p. 17.

NOTE (6)——CONSOLIDATED 3 *per cent*. BANK ANNUITIES. See page 121.—The capital of theſe annuities is made a diſtinct ſtock from that of the annuities called *Reduced*, becauſe it never bore a higher intereſt than 3 *per cent*.—It conſiſted originally of the following loans—37,821*l*. remaining in 1727, of 3 *per cent*. annuities, granted in lieu of St. *Chriſtopher's* and *Nevis* debentures—800,000*l*. borrowed in 1731—600,000*l*. borrowed in 1736——300,000*l*. in 1738——6.400,000*l*. in 1742, 1743, 1744 and 1745, and charged on additional duties on ſpirituous liquors, wines, vinegar, &c.——1.000,000*l*. borrowed in 1750——24.490,000*l*. borrowed in the courſe of the laſt war, and funded on the additional duties on beer, houſes, ſtamps, &c.——4.900,000*l*. borrowed in 1766, 1767 and 1768——And 1.253,700*l*. of the 4 *per cent*. annuities, ſubſcribed into the 3 *per cent*. annuities in 1770.

All theſe loans were by 25 Geo. II. 1751, and ſeveral ſubſequent Acts of Parliament, conſolidated into one joint ſtock; and carried, with the duties for paying the intereſt, to the *Sinking Fund*. And in 1770, they formed a capital of 39.781,521*l*. which has been ſince reduced, by the payments mentioned in the *Poſtſcript* at the end of this tract, to the ſum ſpecified in the account to which this note refers.—See a more full

full account in Mr. Afhmore's Analyfis, &c. from page 5 to page 11.

NOTE (7)——REDUCED 3 *per cent*. BANK ANNUITIES. See page 121.—The capital of thefe annuities confifted, in 1749, of loans in 1746, 1747, and 1748, and navy, ordnance and tranfport debts funded in 1749, amounting to 18.402,472*l*. and all bearing 4 *per cent*. intereft.——By the 23d of Geo. II. 1749, thefe loans were reduced to an intereft of 3 *per cent*. and by the great confolidating Act in 1751, they were converted into one ftock, and carried into the Sinking Fund with the duties on carriages, and the additional duties on glafs, fpirituous liquors, houfes, windows, ftamps, merchandize imported, &c. which had been granted for paying the intereft.— In 1751, certain exchequer tallies and orders, amounting to 129,750*l*. were fubfcribed into this ftock ; and in 1765, navy bills to the amount of 1,482,000*l*. were fubfcribed into it, which made its whole original amount 20.014.222*l*.—— In 1751, there was paid off 830,898*l*. being ftock which had not been fubfcribed agreeably to the Act in 1749 for reducing intereft ; and in 1772, 1774, and 1775, fo much more of this ftock was paid off as reduced it to its prefent amount.— See Mr. Afhmore's Analyfis, p. 12—16.

NOTE (8)——CIVIL LIST MILLION. See page 121.— The income fettled upon King George I. for his civil lift, was 700,000*l*.——In 1720, there had been granted him befides, from the *Royal Exchange* and *London* Affurance companies, 300,000*l*. And in 1726, this million was farther granted towards paying off his debts.

NOTE (9) —— BANK LONG ANNUITY. See page 122. —— This annuity confifts of 128,250*l*. *per ann*. for 99 years, given in 1761, as a *premium* to the fubfcribers of 11.400,000*l*. at 3 *per cent* ; and of 120,000*l*. *per ann*. for 98 years, given in 1762, as a premium to the lenders of twelve millions at 4 *per cent*.

cent. See page 95 and 100. It is charged, together with the loans to which it was annexed, on the *Sinking Fund.* ———— Its value in the Alley is about 25 years purchase; but the remaining term is really worth 27 years purchase, reckoning interest at $3\frac{1}{2}$, (or the 3 *per cents.* being at $85\frac{1}{4}$.) But when interest is at 4 *per cent.* or the 3 *per cents.* are at 75, it is worth only 24 years purchase.——When this annuity is called a *premium*, it must not be imagined, that no compensation was given for it. Government received the value of it; but, at the same time, made itself a debtor for that value. And, what is very surprizing, this has been uniformly practised with respect to all the premiums or douceurs granted by government; and the consequence has been, that great and needless increase of the public debt explained in the 3d section of the 2d Part.

NOTE (10).—SOUTH-SEA STOCK AND ANNUITIES. See page 122.—These four capitals amounting to 25.984,684*l.* 13*s.* consist almost entirely of the remainder of debts contracted in the reigns of *King William* and Queen *Anne.* The following account will probably give sufficient information concerning them.

In 1711, Lord Oxford being minister, the proprietors of certain navy, army, ordnance and transport debts, to the amount of 9.177,968*l.* including arrears of interest, and half a million for the current supplies, were incorporated into a company for trading to the *South-seas.* They were allowed 6 *per cent.* interest for this debt, with 8000*l. per ann.* for management; and the duties on wine, tobacco, *East-India* goods, candles, &c. were made perpetual, and granted as a *Fund* (ever since called the *South-sea Company's Fund*) for paying the interest. This kept up public credit at the time, and has been called the *Earl of Oxford's* master-piece.——By the 1st of Geo. I. 822,032*l.* consisting chiefly of interest payable on the Company's capital, was added to the capital, in consequence of which it was increased to TEN MILLIONS, (ever since called their *original capital*) bearing 6 *per cent.* interest,

interest.——In 1717, they agreed to take 5 *per cent*; and this was the first great reduction of interest, which in conjunction with the same reduction of the other redeemable debts almost all carrying 6 *per cent.* laid the foundation of the SINKING FUND established in this year. But it is remarkable, that so fast did interest fall at this time, that the price of *South-Sea stock*, notwithstanding this reduction, rose from 101 to 111.— In 1719, the *South-Sea* capital was increased to 11.746,844*l.* bearing 5 *per cent.* interest (with an addition of 1,397*l*. 9*s.* to their former allowance for management) by advancing to government 544,142*l.* and by the proprietors of 94,329*l.* 12*s.* lottery annuities for 32 years granted in 1710, accepting in lieu of them 1.202,702*l. South Sea stock.*——In 1720, the agreement was made by government with the South Sea Company, which produced the great SOUTH SEA BUBBLE.—— There existed at that time *long* annuities to the amount of 666,821*l.* 8*s.* and *short* annuities, for 32 years from 1710, to the amount of 127,260*l.* 6*s.* The proprietors of these annuities were allowed to subscribe them into the *South Sea* trading stock; and the Company, for every 100*l.* of the *long* annuity which should be subscribed, were to receive from government an addition to their capital of 2000*l.* bearing 5 *per cent.* interest till 1727, and afterwards 4 *per cent.* till redeemed: and for every 100*l.* of the *short* annuities, they were to receive an addition to their capital of 1400*l.* bearing the same interests.——They were besides to take in the redeemable debts to the amount of 16.546,482*l.* and to receive an addition to their capital of 100*l.* for every 100*l.* subscribed.——By the subscription of the *long* and *short* annuities which followed this agreement, a capital due from government to the Company was created, which was greater by 3.034,769*l.* than the original sum advanced for the annuities subscribed. And as much of these annuities and of the redeemable debts were subscribed, as increased the *South Sea* trading capital to 37.802,203*l.*——In 1722, four millions of this capital was purchased

purchased by the BANK, (See Note 3.) which reduced it to 33.802,203*l*.——By 9 Geo. I. 1723, this remaining capital was divided into two equal parts, one of which alone (or 16.901,101*l*.) was ordered to be the trading capital of the Company, and the other part was directed to be called *South Sea Annuities*.——In 1733, the *South Sea* trading capital had been reduced by payments at different times to 14.651,137*l*. 12*s*. By an Act of Parliament in that year, this remaining stock received a farther division; and only a fourth part, or 3.662,784*l*. was allowed to be the Company's stock; and the other three parts, or 10.988,353*l*. were directed to be called NEW South Sea Annuities, in order to distinguish them from the former annuities, which have ever since gone under the name of OLD South Sea annuities.——From 1733, to the present time, SOUTH SEA STOCK has continued the same; but the capital of the OLD South Sea annuities has been reduced, by redemptions, to 11.907.470*l*. and of the NEW South Sea annuities, to 8.494,830*l*. And of the whole *South Sea* debt, which in 1722 was 33.802,203*l*. there has, since that year, been paid off in all 9.737,119*l*. This should have reduced it to 24.065,081*l*. but it is in reality 25.984,685*l*. The reason of this is, that the diminution just mentioned of the *South Sea* debt was made in part with money borrowed in 1751, to pay off such proprietors of South Sea annuities as had refused to consent to the reduction of interest proposed to them in 1749. The sum borrowed for this purpose was 2.100,000*l*. bearing 3 *per cent*. with 1181*l*. 5*s*. for management. This debt is now reduced by redemptions to the sum specified in the preceding account; or to 1.919,600*l*.

NOTE (11).——EAST-INDIA STOCK. See page 123. ——In 1698, a company of merchants, in consideration of two millions lent to government at 8 *per cent*. were incorporated, and entitled to the sole privilege of trading to the *East-Indies*.——These two millions formed the first capital of the present *East-India* Company.——In 1702, an old company of traders to the *East-Indies* was united to this company; and in

1708, thefe united companies lent to government 1.200,000*l*. without additional intereſt, which made their capital 3.200,000*l*. bearing 5 *per cent.*——In 1730, this intereſt was reduced to, 4 *per cent.* and by the 23d Geo. II. 1749, to 3 *per cent.*—— The falt duties, and fome additional ſtamp duties, were at firſt charged with the annuity due on this capital; but at preſent the duties conſtituting the aggregate fund are charged with it.

NOTE (12).—EAST-INDIA ANNUITY. See page 123.— The capital of this annuity was advanced to government in 1744, at 3 *per cent.* and, in confideration of this loan, the excluſive charter of the Company was continued to Lady-day 1783, at which time it is to ceafe, provided three years notice has been given, and the debt due from government difcharged.

An obfervation here forces itfelf upon me, which I have often had occafion to make.——Part of this loan was a compenfation from the *Eaſt-India* Company for prolonging the term of its charter; and, therefore, ought not to have been included in the loan. The Company would have lent 750,000*l*. on the intereſt common at the time, or 4 *per cent.* and the remainder would have been advanced as a gratuity.— It is a pity thofe who managed thefe contracts for the public, did not attend to the abfurdity and extravagance of making a *debt* of purchafe money, and *borrowing* in the very act of *felling*.

NOTE (13).——EXCHEQUER LONG ANNUITIES. See page 123.——Thefe are the *long* annuities which, in 1720, remained unfubfcribed to the South Sea Company. See Note 10.——They confiſt firſt of annuities to the amount of 54,900*l*. 14*s*. 6*d*. purchafed by the 4th, 5th, and 6th of *William* and *Mary*, for 96 years, from January 1695, with the addition of 1350*l*. *per ann.* for falaries to exchequer officers. Thefe annuities were originally 14 *per cent.* lifeannuities. By the 6th and 7th of *William* and *Mary*, in order to raife more money, thefe annuitants, or any other

perfons

persons for them, were offered a reversionary interest in the annuities after the failure of the lives, till the end of 96 years from January 1695, on paying 4½ years purchase, (that is 63*l*.) for every annuity of 14*l*.——The predecessors of the present company of the MILLION BANK (so called from the MILLION lottery 1694, in which they were some of the principal adventurers) purchased 30,669*l*. 4*s*. of these reversionary annuities. The life annuitants being now reduced to a very small number, almost the whole of this annuity is lapsed to the *company*; and though they have divided for several years 5 *per cent*. on a capital of half a million, yet their growing savings, from the falling in of lives, have been such, that, when their annuity ceases in 1791, they will, I am informed, have accumulated a fund considerably larger, than the capital on which they have made their dividends. But to return.

These EXCHEQUER Annuities consist farther of

£.	s.	d.	
30,400	6	8	purchased for 99 years from *Christmas* 1705, by 2d and 3d of *Anne*, with 1450*l*. for management.
23,234	16	6	purchased for 99 years from *Lady-day*, 1706, by 4 *Anne*, with 1470*l. per ann.* for management.
7,776	10	0	purchased for 99 years from *Lady-day*, 1707, by 5 *Anne*, with 375*l*. 12*s. per ann.* for management.
4,710	0	0	purchased for 99 years from *Lady-day*, 1708, by 6th of *Anne*, with 208*l*. 2*s. per ann.* for management.
10,181	0	0	purchased for 99 years from *Lady-day*, 1707, by a 2d Act of 5th of *Anne*, with 416*l. per ann.* for management.
Add 54,900	14	6	
131,203	7	8	Total.

The original sum contributed for these annuities was 1,836,276*l*. They are even now worth more than this sum. The public has already paid above TEN MILLIONS; and by the time they are all extinct, it will have paid above THIRTEEN MILLIONS, on their account. This is great extravagance; but it is nothing to the extravagance constantly practised of borrowing on perpetual annuities, without putting them into a fixed course of redemption.

NOTE (14).—TONTINE by an act of 6 Geo. III. See page 124.—The intention of this Act was to raise 300,000*l*. towards paying off navy bills, by offering to subscribers for every 100*l*. advanced, an annuity of 3*l*. for their lives, with benefit of survivorship. But the scheme did not succeed, and only 18000*l*. was subscribed.

NOTE (15).——LIFE ANNUITIES. See page 124.—— The annuities on *two* lives in 1694, were sold at 12*l*. *per ann*. during *two* lives, of any ages, and the annuities on *three* lives, at 10*l*. *per ann*. during *three* lives, for every 100*l*. advanced. ——-This was very extravagant; for, supposing the annuitants in general, about the age of 20 or 30, it was the same, in the case of *two* lives, with giving above 10 *per cent*. for money, and in the case of three lives, 9 *per cent*.—— It is, likewise, extremely absurd in these cases to pay no regard to difference of ages. A *single* life at the age of 60, supposing money improved at 4 *per cent*. is intitled to 11 *per cent*. but at the age of 10, scarcely to 6 *per cent*. *Two* lives at 60, are entitled, on the same supposition, to $8\frac{1}{2}$ *per cent*. but at 10, not to 5 *per cent*.——The original amount of these annuities was 22,700*l*. nearly. In 1762, that is, in 68 years, they were reduced by deaths no lower than 9,215*l*.

The other life-annuities mentioned in the preceding account were *douceurs* granted for loans in 1745, 1746, and 1757. An account of the annuities granted in the last of these years may be seen in page 101.

The life-annuities in 1745, amounted to 22,500*l*. and were granted, together with the profits of a lottery, for a loan of two millions at 4 *per cent*.

The life-annuities in 1746, amounted to 45,000*l.* and were granted, with the profits of another lottery, for a loan of three millions, at the same interest.——The remarks made in the 3d section of the last part, and particularly in the note, p. 101, are applicable to these two loans. The value of the life-annuities, and the profits of the lotteries, were made a part of the public debt. And, supposing the life-annuities worth, one with another, only 14 years purchase, and the profits of the two lotteries worth 300,000*l.* it will follow, that the capital created by these loans, instead of being 5,000,000*l.* should have been only 3,755,000*l.*

But there is another remark, which it is proper to mention here. The life-annuities granted in 1757, amounting to 33,750*l.* were, in January 1775, that is in 18 years, reduced by deaths to 28,732*l.* or but a little more than a seventh part. But, supposing the annuitants all in the firmest stage of life, or between the age of 10 and 30, they ought, according to some of the best tables of observations, to have been reduced a *quarter*. These life-annuities have, therefore, fallen in much more slowly than could have been expected; and I have found the same to be true of all the other life-annuities.——The reason, undoubtedly, is, that the tables exhibit the rate of mortality among all sorts and orders of men taken together; whereas, the lives on which annuities are bought, are a selection of the better sort of lives from the general mass, and therefore must be of greater value.——Indeed I am not acquainted with any table of observations which gives the probabilities of the duration of life high enough to be a guide in this case; except that which was formed by Mr. *De Parcieux*, from the French *Tontines.*——A calculation, therefore, of the values of lives, agreeably to this table, would be of considerable use.

NOTE (16).——UNFUNDED DEBT. See page 124.——
I have given the navy debt, as it was in January, 1775.—
The civil list debt in 1775, was probably more than the sum at which I have reckoned it. Lord STAIR, in his account of the national debt, income, and expenditure, reckons it at 800,000*l.*

Much the greateſt part of the foregoing debts, with the taxes for paying the intereſt, including the duties compoſing the *Aggregate, South-Sea,* and *General* Funds, have, by the 25th of *George* the Second, 1751, and ſeveral ſubſequent acts of Parliament, been thrown into one general account; and the *ſurplus* of the whole, after deducting the intereſt, 800,000 l. *per ann.* to the civil liſt, and a few other payments, forms the SINKING FUND.——The debts not brought to this account are about ſeven millions and a half in the *South-Sea* Houſe; 11.186,800 l. of the *Bank* capital; the Civil Liſt million; four millions and a half borrowed at 3½ *per cent.* in 1758; the capital of the Eaſt-India annuity; and the Exchequer long and life annuities, except thoſe granted in 1758. But the *ſurpluſſes* of the duties which pay the intereſt of theſe debts are either carried *immediately* into the *Sinking Fund* account; or brought *firſt* to the *Aggregate* Fund, and from thence carried into that account.——On the contrary. Deficiencies in theſe duties when they happen, are made good out of the Sinking Fund; and afterwards replaced from the ſupplies.

For example. Three old nine-penny exciſes on beer, with an additional three-pence per barrel, producing above half a million annually; alſo, 3,700 l. *per* week out of the hereditary exciſe on beer,

beer, together with some duties on paper, coals, &c. and ⅓ additional subsidy of tonnage and poundage, are appropriated to the payment of the Banker's Annuity; the Life Annuities granted in 1693 and 1694; the Exchequer Long Annuities; and annuities on various sums subscribed to the South-Sea Company in 1720. The surplusses make a part of the *Aggregate Fund*; and after contributing to satisfy the charge on that fund, are carried into the *Sinking Fund.*——— Again. Certain additional duties on soap, parchment, coals, &c. are appropriated to pay the interest of 1.250,000l. and of 1.750,000l. parts of the Bank capital.——The surplusses are carried *directly* to the *Sinking Fund.*——In like manner. The duties on houses and windows imposed by an act of the 20th of *George* the Second, 1747, (*a*) after deducting from them 91,485 l. *per ann.* to satisfy certain charges on old houseduties in the *Aggregate Fund*; and, also, other duties on houses and windows imposed by the 2d and 6th of *George* the Third, amounting in all to about 205,000l. *per ann.* are carried into the Sinking Fund, together with the capitals, the in-

---

(*a*) These duties were appropriated to the payment of the interest at 4 *per cent.* of a capital of 4.400,000l. created in 1747, for which four millions only had been advanced. It is now a part of the capital of the reduced 3 *per cent.* annuities.

terest

tereſt of which has been charged upon them. But the addition to theſe duties (with a tax on penſions) granted in 1758, and charged with the intereſt (at 3 ½ per cent.) of the loan in that year, having not been carried into the *Sinking Fund*, and proving deficient; the deficiency is conſtantly made good out of this fund, and afterwards replaced from the ſupplies.

State and Amount of the NATIONAL DEBT *at Chriſtmas* 1753; *with the Charges of Management.*

BANK OF ENGLAND.

	Principal. £.	Intereſt. £.
BANK capital	11.686,800	393,038
Of this capital 3.200,000l. bore at this time 3 per cent. intereſt; and the remainder bore 3 ½ per cent. till 1757, by 23d Geo. II. 1749.——See note (1) p. 125. Management 5,898l. per ann.		
Three *per cent.* BANK Annuities conſolidated by 25 Geo. II. 1751.—See note (6) p. 127. Management 4,450l. per ann.	9.137,821	274,135
Total	£20.824,621	667,173

BANK

	Principal. £.	Interest. £.
Brought over	20.824,621	667,173
BANK Annuities consolidated by 25 Geo. II. 2.713,618 l. carrying 3¼ per cent. interest till 1755; and 14.857,956 l. carrying the same interest till 1757. See note (7) p. 128.	17,7401,32	619,546
Management 9,884 l. per ann.		
Civil List million, 1726	1.000,000	30,000
Management 360 l. per ann. Whole charge of Management at the Bank in 1753—20,592 l. per ann.		
SOUTH-SEA COMPANY. SOUTH-SEA Stock carrying 4 per cent. till 1757	3.662,784	146,511
Old and New SOUTH-SEA Annuities carrying 3½ per cent. till 1757	21.362,525	747,688
Three per cent. 1751— See note (10) p. 131.	2.100,000	63,000
Whole charge of management at the *South-Sea-House* on stock and annuities, 15,748 l. per ann.		
EAST-INDIA HOUSE. EAST-INDIA STOCK, reduced to 3½ till 1757	3.200,000	112,000
	£.69.851,254	2.385,918

EAST

	Principal.	Interest.
	£.	£.
Brought over	69.851,254	2.385,918
EAST-INDIA annuity 1744	1.000,000	30,000
Management 1,687l. 10s. *per ann.*		

| Total (a) | £.70,851,254 | 2.415,918 |

(a) The whole of this sum, (except 16.437,821l. consisting of the old Bank capital, the consolidated 3 *per cents*, the South-Sea 3 *per cent.* annuities 1751, the Civil List million, and the East-India annuity) that is, 54.413,433l. was reduced by 23 Geo. II. 1749, from an interest of 4 *per cent.* to 3 ½ till 1757, and afterwards to 3 *per cent.*——The proprietors of a capital of 3.290,042l. refused to consent to this reduction, which, therefore, was paid off; 1.190,042l. with *Exchequer* Bills (afterwards cancelled) ; and 2.100,000l. with money borrowed at 3 *per cent.* and added to the capital of the *South-Sea* annuities. The whole sum, therefore, reduced and paid off, was 57.703,475l. which produced a saving to the public, and an addition to the Sinking Fund after 1757, of 612,735l. *per ann.*

The SALT DUTIES in 1753 had been for some time mortgaged to pay the principal and interest of a million borrowed in 1745. In 1757, after clearing the mortgage, they became free, and were carried into the Sinking Fund, of which they have ever since formed a part. This produced a farther addition to the *Sinking Fund*, after 1757, of about 220,000 l. *per ann.*

I have not included the million now mentioned in the account given above of the public debts in 1753, because it was in a fixed course of redemption ; nor have I included 499,600l. in Exchequer Bills charged on the duty on sweets, because these Exchequer Bills were paid off in 1754.

EXCHEQUER

	Principal. £.	Interest. £.
Brought over	70,851,254	2,415,918

EXCHEQUER.

ANNUITIES for 96 and 99 years from various dates in King *William*'s and Queen *Anne*'s times being the original sum contributed. See note (13) page 132. — 1,836,276 | 131,203

Management 5,230l. *per ann.* inclusive of management for the two next articles.

ANNUITIES for lives with benefit of survivorship, being the original sum contributed — 108,100 | 7,567

ANNUITIES for two and three lives, being the remainder after deducting the annuities fallen in by deaths, and reckoned worth 10 years purchase — — 106,650 | 10,665

ANNUITIES for single lives 1745, being the remainder after deducting the annuities fallen in by deaths; and reckoned worth 14 years purchase — — 296,142 | 21,153

£.73,198,422 | 2,586,506

	Principal. £.	Interest. £.
Brought over	73,198,422	2,586,506
ANNUITIES for single lives 1746, being the remainder after the lives fallen in	582,274	41,591
Navy debt in 1754—Interest reckoned at 2 per cent.	1,296,568	25,931
Total of the principal and interest of the public debts in 1753	£.75,077,264	2,654,028

STATE and AMOUNT of the NATIONAL DEBT in 1739.

BANK OF ENGLAND.

	Principal. £.	Interest. £.
BANK CAPITAL, consisting of 1,600,000l. old capital carrying 6 per cent; and 7,500,000l. carrying 4 per cent. See note 1, p. 123.	9,100,000	396,000
BANK ANNUITIES at 3 per cent. for the lottery in 1731.	800,000	24,000
	£.9,900,000	420,000

SOUTH-

	Principal. £.	Interest. £.
Brought over	623,312	2.321,215
SOUTH-SEA COMPANY. Stock and annuities bearing 4 *per cent.*	27.302,203	1.092,088
EAST-INDIA COMPANY. EAST-INDIA stock carrying 4 *per cent.*	3.200,000	128,000
EXCHEQUER ANNUITIES. Annuities at 3 ½ by 4 Geo. II. paid off in 1752	400,000	14,000
ANNUITIES at 4 *per cent.* charged on the duty on wrought plate by 6 Geo. I. 1720	312,000	12,480
182,250 l. of this capital was paid off in 1750. The remainder is now included in the capital of the reduced 3 *per cent.* annuities.		
ANNUITIES at 3 *per cent.* charged on the Sinking Fund by 9 and 10 Geo. II. Now included in the confolidated 3 *per cent.* annuities	900,000	27,000
ANNUITIES on *Nevis* and St. *Christopher* Debentures at 3 *per cent.* Now included in the confolidated 3 *per cents.*	37,821	1,135
	£.42.052,024	1.694,703

EXCHEQUER

	Principal. £.	Interest. £.
Brought over	42,052,024	1,694,703
EXCHEQUER BILLS charged on a duty upon victuallers by 12 Geo. I. 1726—Carrying 3 per cent. — —	480,000	14,400
EXCHEQUER BILLS charged on a duty on sweets by 10 of Geo. II. 1737— Carrying 3 per cent. and paid off in 1754—See the note p. 140. —	499,600	14,988
ANNUITIES for long terms from various dates —	1,836,276	131,203
ANNUITIES for lives with benefit of *Survivorship* granted in 1693	108,100	7,567
ANNUITIES for two and three lives, 1694 —	106,650	15,000
Navy debt *(a)* —	1,300,000	26,000
Total of the *Principal* and *Interest* of the National Debt in 1739 *(b)*	£.46,382,650	1,903,861

(*a*) Having met with no account of the Navy Debt at this time, I have chosen, rather than omit it, to suppose it nearly the same that it was at the commencement of the last war; which, probably, is reckoning it too high.

(*b*) In this account I have omitted a million borrowed in 1734, because the redemption of it was near being completed by the Salt Duties. I have also omitted *Short Annuities* amounting to 24,334l. being the remainder of 9 *per cent.* annuities for 32 years created in 1710, because the term for which they were created was near expiring.

From

From the account in the POSTSCRIPT, at the end of this tract, it will appear, that 10.639,793l. of the public debt was discharged between the years 1763 and 1775; and also that the *funded* debt was, in 1775, 1,400,000l. greater than it was at the end of the last war. From hence, and from the amount of the public debt in 1775, as stated in page 124, it follows, that the funded debt at the end of the war was 130.943,051 l. and the whole debt 146.582,844l. and, consequently, that the war left upon the nation an *unfunded debt* amounting to (a) 15.639,793l. This unfunded debt consisted of the following particulars—Of 3,500,000l. borrowed after the peace in 1763, and applied towards bearing such expences of the war as could not immediately cease with its operations. ——Of near *eight millions* in navy, victualling, ordnance, and transport debts.——Of 1.800,000l.

(a) The author of the *Considerations on the Trade and Finances of this Kingdom* makes this debt 1.318,000 l. more than the sum at which I have here stated it. See page 22; and *State of the Nation* by the same auther, page 15, quarto editions.——The reason of this difference is, that this writer has included in the unfunded debt left by the war the deficiencies of grants and funds in 1763 and 1764, and the *whole* army debt not provided for in those years; whereas I have excluded the former entirely; and admitted only as much of the latter as exceeded the army debts common in subsequent years. See the Postscript.

L. Exchequer

Exchequer bills; and the remainder, of fubfidies to foreign princes, extraordinaries of the army, and German demands.

In the interval of peace between 1748 and 1755 the following debts were paid off.

	£.
Bank Annuities bearing 4 *per cent.*	1,013,148
SOUTH-SEA Annuities bearing 4 *per cent.*	176,893
Annuities bearing $3\frac{1}{2}$ *per cent.* charged by 4 Geo. II. on additional Stamp-duties	400,000
EXCHEQUER Bills bearing 3 *per cent.* charged by 10 Geo. II. 1737 on the duties on fweets	499,600
Borrowed in 1745 at $3\frac{1}{2}$ *per cent.* on the credit of the Salt duties See note, page 140.	1,000,000

(*a*) Total £.3,089,641

(*b*) In 1751 there was applied to the payment of Navy debts 200,000l. and in 1752, the fum of 900,000l. But I have not reckoned thefe fums, becaufe they did little more than make up the conftant deficiency in the *Peace Eftablifhment* for the Navy.

From

From the whole, the following account of the progress of the National Debt, from 1739 to 1775, may be deduced.

	Principal £.	Interest. £.
Amount of the *principal* and *interest* of the national debt before the war which begun in 1740	46,382,650	1,903,861
Amount in 1749 immediately after the war	78,166,906	2,765,608
Increased by the war	31,784,256	861,747
Diminished by the Peace from 1748 to 1755	3,089,641	111,590
Amount at the commencement of the last war	75,077,264	2,654,018
Amount at the end of the war in 1763	146,582,844	4,840,821
Increased by the last war	71,505,580	2,186,803
Diminished by the Peace, in twelve years from 1763 to 1775	10,639,793	(a) 400,000
Amount at *Midsummer*, 1775	135,943,051	4,440,821

We are now involved in another war, and the public debts are increasing again fast. *Exchequer* Bills have been increased from 1,250,000l. to 1,500,000l. A new capital of 2,150,000l. has been added to the 3 *per cent*. Consolidated An-

(*a*) See the Postscript.

nuities. And a vote of credit was given in the laſt feſſion of Parliament for a million. The laſt year, therefore, has added 3.400,0col. to our debts, befides a vaſt ſum not yet provided for, confifting of navy, ordnance, victualling, tranfport and army debts.——The prefent year (1777) muſt make another great addition to them; and what they will be at the end of thefe troubles, no one can tell.——The union of a *foreign* war to the prefent *civil* war might perhaps raife them to Two HUNDRED MILLIONS; but, more probably, it would fink them to——NOTHING.

S E C T. III.

Of the DEBTS *and* RESOURCES *of France*.

MINISTERS have of late fought to remove the public apprehenfions by general accounts of the weaknefs of powers, which, from the circumftances of former wars as well as national prejudices, have been felt by the people as jealous rivals or formidable enemies.——I wifh it was poffible for me to confirm thefe accounts; and by contrafting the preceding ftate of our own debts with a fimilar one of thofe of FRANCE, to fhew, that from this power in particular we have nothing to fear. The following particulars, on
the

the correctness of which I can rely, may give some assistance in judging of this subject.

The whole expence of the last war to FRANCE was 1.113.307,047 livres; that is, 49.702,000 l. sterling. of which 23.152,000 l. (520.926,000 livres) consisted of money procured by the sale of taxes, by free-gifts, and extra-impositions during the war, which left behind them no debts: And 26.550,000 l. (597.380,100 livres) consisted of LOANS, or money raised on perpetual annuities, life-annuities, and lotteries.—At the beginning of 1769 the whole amount of the debts of *France*, including all arrears and capitals advanced on annuities and lotteries, was 128.622,000 l. sterling, or 2.894.053,616 livres. The annual charge derived from this debt was 6.707,500 l. sterling (150.919,284 livres)——All the appropriations amounted to 8.218,500 l. sterling (184.919,284 livres).——The expences of the army, navy, king's houshold, prince's houshold, foreign affairs, &c. amounted to 8.947,000 l. or 201.307,312 livres. So that the whole annual expence was 17.165,000 l. (386.226,596 livres).--The whole revenue had amounted, before 1769, to 13.484.500 l. sterling (303.401,696 livres).——The public expence, therefore, had exceeded the revenue 3.681,000 l. (82.800,000 livres) *per ann.*

From the year 1769 to the prefent King's Acceffion, by forced reductions of intereft, and by new taxes, the public revenue was carried to 16.289,000 l. fterling (366.508,000 livres) and the public expence was reduced fo as not to exceed the revenue above 766,800 l. *per annum* (17.253,000 livres).——The anticipations alfo of the revenue, which before 1769 had extended to *feventeen* months, were reduced to *five* months.— Such was the progrefs of reformation; namely, an increafe of revenue amounting to little lefs than THREE MILLIONS fterling *per ann.* in a few years, under an unpopular minifter, in the latter days of a reign never characterized by an attention to oeconomy, or a regard to the public intereft; and at this time particularly ftamped by unprecedented profufion and a general relaxation.

A new reign produced a new minifter of finance whofe name will be refpected by pofterity for a fet of meafures as new to the *political* world, as any late difcoveries in the fyftem of nature have been to the *philofophical* world.—Doubtful in their operation, as all unproved meafures muft be, but diftinguifhed by their tendency to lay a folid foundation for endlefs peace, induftry, and a general enjoyment of the gifts of nature, arts, and commerce.——The edicts iffued during his adminiftration exhibit indeed a phænomenon of the moft extraordinary kind. An abfolute king rendering

dering a voluntary account to his subjects, and inciting his people to *think*; a right which it has been the business of all absolute princes and their ministers to extinguish in the minds of men.——In these edicts the King declared in the most distinct terms against a bankruptcy, an augmentation of taxes, and new loans; while the minister applied himself to increase every public resource by principles more liberal than *France*, or any part of *Europe*, ever had in serious contemplation.——It is much to be regretted that the intrigues of a court, want of address, or perhaps want of due regard to that degree of public conviction, which must influence more or less in a despotic as well as free state, should have deprived the world of those lights which must have resulted from the example of such an administration.

After a short interval, a nomination, in some respects still more extraordinary, has taken place in the court of FRANCE. A court which a few years since was distinguished by its bigotry and intolerance, has raised a *Protestant*, the subject of a small but virtuous republic, to a decisive lead in the regulation of its finances. It is to be presumed, that so singular a preference will produce an equally singular exertion of integrity and talents. Though differing from Monsieur TURGOT in several principles, which regard the larger lines of government, he appears by his first steps, and, particularly, the preamble to a late edict for raising 24 millions of livres by a lottery, to put his foot on the same great basis of general justice, and a strict conservation of the faith of the king; and points more particularly at the surest of all resources in any modern states, a simplification of taxes and a reformation in the collection of them. This administration, making improvements in the Revenue its immediate object, is more capable of present exertion; and, as such, is more formidable.

From these facts and observations it is impossible not to conclude, that if we trust our safety to the difficulties of FRANCE, we may find ourselves fatally deceived. I will add, that though (like the 3 s. land-tax and lotteries among ourselves) some of the extraordinary impositions of the last war have been continued in *France*, there are some which ceased with the war, and which they can renew. It is, particularly, an advantage of unspeakable importance to them, that they can carry on a war, as they did the last, at *half* our expence; and that, having no dependence on the flattering delusion of paper, they can, as they did in 1759, bear even a bankruptcy in the middle of a war, and yet carry it on vigorously.—Their debts time itself is sinking fast. Of 3.111,000 l. (seventy millions of livres) in annuities on the *Hotel de Ville* at *Paris* 1.777,000 l. (forty millions of livres) consisted in 1774 of Life Annuities, which were falling by deaths at the rate of 71,000l. (1.600,000 livres) every year.——Even their lofs of credit, whatever prefent embarraffment attends it, favours them upon the whole. To this they owe the advantages juft mentioned. The facility with which our high credit has enabled us to run in debt enfnares us; and, if a change of meafures does not take place, *(a)* muft *ruin* us. Experience has given them a juft horror at borrowing on permanent funds; and were they inclined to do it, they are not able to do it to any great amount; and, confequently, they cannot go on mortgaging one refource after another till none is left.—While we lofe fight of the capital in the intereft, they carry their views chiefly to the reimburfement of the capital; and after receiving high intereft, for fome years, can be fatisfied with receiving back a part of their capital.——Their debts, being confined in a great meafure to the *Farmers General* and others at PARIS, are not circulated and diffufed among the body of the people in the manner ours are: And it is well known, that they can make ufe of methods to difcharge them which our government muft never think of. The acts of arbitrary power and unjuft expedients to which, on many occa-

---

(a) " Either the nation (Mr. Hume fays) muft deftroy " public credit, or public credit will deftroy the nation." Political Effays, page 135.

fions,

fions, they have had recourfe for this purpofe without producing any tumults, are fuch as appear to us almoft incredible; and fhould the time ever come, when it will be neceffary in this country to make ufe of any violence of the fame kind, all government will probably be at an end.

In point of territory and number of inhabitants, the two countries will bear no comparifon *(a)*. We have hitherto oppofed *France* by our free fpirit, and our colonies; and to them chiefly we owe our profperity and victories. Our colonies, once feparated from us, the iflands will foon follow. But fhould they remain ours, our comparative advantages will beft appear from the following authentic account of the imports into *France* from their iflands.

In 1774.

	Weight in Pounds.
Sugar imported into *France* —	147.986,959
Indigo — — —	1.734,206
Rocou — — —	210,187
Coffee — — —	58.247,133
	208.178,485

(a) The number of inhabitants in *France* is 26 millions. In *Britain* it cannot exceed fix or feven millions. See p. 66. And *Obfervations on Reverfionary Payments*, page 185, third edition.

In

In 1775.

	Weight in Pounds.
Sugar imported into *France* —	171.932,972
Indigo — — —	2.134,247
Rocou — — —	169,831
Coffee — — —	58.545,000
	(*a*) 232.782,050

Value of the above commodities re-exported from *France*, taken upon the average price.

	Livres.	*Sterling.*
In 1774 —	75.901,373 —	3.373,000
In 1775 —	74.961,318 —	3.331,000

The whole importation from the *West-Indies* into *Britain* is about three millions *per ann.*

But I have gone much beyond the views with which I begun this section. The facts which have been stated, and the reflections which they have occasioned, are intended principally to shew that we ought not to suffer ourselves to be drawn into security by any assurances of the weakness of *France.* — May she, however, find herself the weakest of kingdoms whenever, from motives of

(*a*) Near one half of all this importation is made into *Bourdeaux* only; and the rest into *Rochelle, Marseilles, Nantz, Havre,* and *Honfleur.*

interest

intereſt or ambition, ſhe ſhall attempt to injure any of her neighbours.———May *Britain*, hitherto the moſt favoured ſpot under heaven, always preſerve her diſtinguiſhed happineſs, and eſcape the danger which now threatens her. And may the time ſoon come, when all mankind, ſenſible of the value of the bleſſings of peace and equal liberty, ſhall ſuffer one another to enjoy them, and learn war no more.

SECT. IV.

Containing the Corrections and Additions in the different Editions of the Obſervations on Civil Liberty, *with Remarks on the* EARL OF STAIR's *Account of the National Income and Expenditure.*

ALL the corrections and additions, of the leaſt conſequence, in the different editions of the *Obſervations on Civil Liberty*, are confined to the APPENDIX; and the proprietors of any of the editions of that pamphlet will be poſſeſſed of it in all the correctneſs that I have been capable of giving it, by ſtriking out, in the four firſt editions, the account in p. 115. of the national income and expenditure; and by ſubſtituting, in all the editions, the preceeding account of the national debt, and alſo the

ful-following accounts (*a*), in the room of accounts correfponding to them, in page 119, and page 123, &c. of the four firft editions, and in page 115, 118, &c. and 123, &c. of the fubfequent octavo editions.

APPROPRIATED REVENUE *at Midfummer*, 1775.

	£.
Intereft of the national debt —	4.440,821
Civil lift revenue — —	800,000
Expences of management attending the national debt; of which 71,432 l. is the expence of management at the Bank, South-Sea Houfe, and *India* Houfe; and 5.900 l. falaries to *Exchequer Officers*. See Page 119, &c. —	77,332
Annuities payable out of the Aggregate Fund to the DUKE OF GLOUCESTER, 8000 l.—DUKE OF CUMBERLAND, 8000 l.—the Reprefentatives of ARTHUR ONSLOW, Efq; 3000 l.—And the Sheriffs of ENGLAND and WALES, 4000 l.—In all	23,000

(*a*) The chief difference between thefe accounts is, that thofe which follow are, in fome inftances, more full; and enlarged by references to *Lord Stair's* accounts.

Clerk

Clerk of the Hanaper in Chancery,— Coinage (*a*) expence——Tenths and firſt-fruits of the Clergy ap- propriated to the augmentation of ſmall livings—Extra revenues of the crown, conſiſting of *American* quit-rents; duty of $4\frac{1}{2}$ per cent. in the Leeward Iſlands; revenues of Gibraltar and dutchy of *Cornwall*, &c.—Fees for warrants and orders, for auditing and engroſſing accounts of dividend warrants, and other charges at the EXCHEQUER and TREASURY (*b*) —— —— 100,000

Total of the Appropriated Revenue £. 5,441,153

(*a*) In order to defray the expence of coinage, a duty of 10s. per ton has been laid on wines imported; and, as far as this duty happens to fall ſhort of 15,000l, the deficiency is made good out of the ſupplies.

(*b*) I am not able to give the exact amount of this part of the appropriated revenue. I have, therefore, reckoned it at ſuch a round ſum, as, I think, cannot much exceed or fall ſhort of it.

· *State*

State of the SURPLUS of the REVENUE for 11 years ended at 1775.

UNAPPROPRIATED REVENUE.

NEAT PRODUCE of the Sinking Fund, for five years, including casual surplusses, reckoning to *Christmas* in every year; being the annual medium, after deducting from it about 45,000 l. always carried to it from the supplies, in order to replace so much taken from it every year to make good a deficiency in a Fund established in 1758. — — £. 2.610,759

Neat annual produce of Land Tax at 3s. militia deducted; and of the Malt Tax *(a)* — — 1.800,000

(N. B. These two taxes in 1773, brought in only 1.665,475 l.)

There are some casual Receipts, not included in the Sinking Fund, such as Savings in Pay-Office, duties on Gum Senega, American Revenue, &c. But they are so uncertain and inconsiderable, that it is scarcely proper to give them as a part of the permanent Revenue. Add however on this account — 50,000

Total of unappropriated Revenue £. 4.460,759

(a) The Land-tax at 3 s. is given by Parliament for 1.500,000 l.; and the Malt-tax for 750,000 l. but they are always greatly deficient.—Both these taxes (and also sometimes the income of the Sinking Fund) are borrowed of the *Bank*, and spent long before they come into the Exchequer; and therefore, are debts constantly due to the Bank, for which interest is paid.

Produce

Produce of the SINKING FUND, *reckoned to* Chriftmas *in every Year.*

1770	£.2.486,836
1771	2.553,505
1772	2.683,831
1773	2.823,150
1774	2.731,476

The average of thefe five years is 2.655,759 l. or, deducting 45,000 l. (as directed in the laft page), 2.610,759 l.

In 1775, the Sinking Fund was taken for 2.900,000 l. including an extraordinary charge of 100,000 l. on the *Aggregate* Fund; but it produced 2.917,869 l. The average of fix years, including 1775, was 2.654,443 l. The average of five years before 1770, was 2.234,780 l.

ANNUAL EXPENDITURE.

	£.
Peace Eftablifhment, for the Navy and Army, including all mifcellaneous and incidental expences	3.700,000
Annual increafe of the Navy and Civil Lift debts — —	350,000
Intereft at 2 *per cent.* of 3.600,000 l. unfunded debt, which muft be paid out of the unappropriated Revenue — — —	72,000
Total	4.122,000
ANNUAL SURPLUS of the Revenue	338,759
Annual income £.	4.460,759

The

The estimate for the peace establishment, including miscellaneous expences, amounted, in 1775, to 3,703,476 l.—But the extraordinary expences, occasioned by the war with America, made it fall very short.—In 1774 it amounted to 3,784,452 l. exclusive of 250,000 l. raised by Exchequer Bills, towards defraying the expence of calling in the gold coin. And the medium for eleven years, from 1765, has been nearly 3,700,000 l. — According to the accounts which I have collected, the expence of the peace establishment (including miscellaneous expences) was in 1765, 1766, and 1767, 3,540,000 l. *per ann.*—In 1768, 1769, and 1770, it was 3,354,000 l. *per ann.*—— In 1771, 1772, 1773, 1774, and 1775, the average has been nearly four millions *per ann.* exclusive of the expence of calling in the coin.

The parliament votes for the sea service 4 l. *per* month *per* man, including wages, wear and tear, victuals and ordnance. This allowance is insufficient, and falls short every year more or less, in proportion to the number of men voted. From hence, in a great measure, arises that annual increase of the navy debt, mentioned in the second article of the *National Expenditure*. This increase in 1772 and 1773 was 669,996 l. or 335,000 l. *per ann.* The number of men voted in those two years, was 20,000. I have supposed them reduced to 16,000, and the annual increase of the Navy

Debt to be only 250,000 l.———Add 100,000 l. for the annual increase of the Civil Lift Debt, and the total will be 350,000 l.

Soon after the publication of the preceding account in *February* last year, the EARL OF STAIR obliged the public with another account of the same kind, which brings out a conclusion much more unfavourable. According to this account, were lotteries abolished, and the land-tax at 3s. in the pound only, there would be a *deficiency* in the revenue, instead of such a *surplus* as I have stated. The following remarks will shew the reason of this difference.

The EARL OF STAIR has taken the annual produce of the *Sinking* Fund at 2,506,400 l. being the average produce of EIGHT years ended at *Lady day* 1775 ——I have taken it at 2,610,759 l. being the average of FIVE years ended at *Christmas* 1775.——The neat produce of the land and malt taxes has been also taken near 50,000 l. higher in my account; and I have besides admitted 50,000 l. *per ann.* for casual supplies, which his Lordship has not charged.

The annual increase of the Navy Debt, LORD STAIR states at 300,000 l. and of the Civil Lift at 200,000 l. I have stated the former at 250,000 l. and the latter at 100,000 l.—In order also to avoid, as much as possible, all exaggeration, I have thrown out the expence of the new coinage. Lord Stair has admitted it, and given an yearly expence derived from hence of 100,000 l.—— He has also taken the Peace Eftablishment for 1774, as a fair medium for common years of peace, becaufe it was lower in that year than in the three years preceding 1775. I have taken the average of *eleven* years of peace, which is 75,000 l. lefs.

In confequence of thefe differences, the national PEACE expenditure in *Lord Stair*'s account comes out 325,000 l. *per ann.* higher than in mine; and the national income comes out 204,359 l. *lower*; from whence it follows, that without lotteries, and the land being at 3 s. in the pound, the kingdom muft, according to his Lordfhip's calculation, run out at the rate of about 200,000l. every year.

In fome of the particulars I have mentioned, this account is probably neareft to the truth; but, I hope, it will be confidered, that I have ftudied to give moderate accounts, and aimed at erring always rather on the favourable than the unfavourable fide.

Second Method of deducing the SURPLUS *of the* REVENUE.

From the year 1763 to the year 1775, or during a period of 12 years, 10.639,793 l. of the public (*a*) debt was paid off.—The money employed for

(*a*) The account given by Lord North at opening the Budget in 1775, was, that the public debt had been diminifhed fince 1763, near nine millions and a half. The grounds on which I have ftated this diminution at 10.639,793 l. may be feen in the POSTSCRIPT, p. 171.

this purpofe muft have been derived from the furplus of the *ordinary* revenue, added to the *extraordinary* receipts. Thefe receipts have confifted of the following articles.——1ft. The land-tax at 4s. in the pound in 1764, 1765, 1766, and 1771; or 1s. in the pound extraordinary for four years, making 1.750,000l.——2. The profits of ten lotteries (*a*) making (at 150,000l. each lottery) 1.500,000l.——3. A contribution of 400,000l. *per ann.* for five years from the EAST INDIA Company, making 2.000,000l.——4. Savings by debts difcharged at a difcount, (*b*) making at leaft 400,000l.——5. Paid by the Bank in 1764 for the renewal of their charter, 110,000l.—6. Savings on high grants during the war; produce of *French* prizes taken before the declaration of war; fale of lands in the ceded iflands; and compofition for maintaining *French* prifoners, (*c*) making 2.520,000l.

(*a*) Four of thefe lotteries have been annexed to annuities; but it would be a great miftake to think that they have not been equally profitable with the other lotteries. For inftance; in 1767, a million and a half was borrowed on an annuity of 45,000l. with a lottery of 60,000 tickets annexed. In the fame year, 2.616,777l. was paid off; but, had it not been for the lottery, only 1.350,000l. could have been raifed on the annuity; and 150,000l. lefs muft have been paid off.

(*b*) The difcounts on a million and a half paid off in 1772, and two millions paid off in 1774 and 1775, amounted nearly to this fum.

(*c*) The particular fums may be found in a pamphlet, entitled, *The Prefent State of the Nation*, p. 28, quarto edition.

2,520,000 l. ———— All these sums amount to 8,280,000l. There remains to make up 10,639,793 l. (the whole debt discharged) 2,359,793 l. and this, therefore, is the amount of the whole surplus of the *ordinary* revenue for twelve years; or 196,000l. per ann. *(b)*

The Earl of STAIR has also, in this method, calculated the *surplus* of the Revenue; and makes the total, for eleven years, to be no more than 2,557,378 l. even with the assistance of lotteries, and the land-tax at 4s. in the pound for five years; from whence it follows, that *without* these assistances, there would have been a deficiency of near 60,000 l. *per ann.*—The reason is, that his Lordship has taken the whole debt paid since 1763, at no more than 7,053,855 l. or three millions and a half less than I have made it; and he has taken it so much less, chiefly in consequence of including in the amount of the public debt in 1775, the excess of the expences of that year above the common peace expences. This excess is to be charged to the present war; and, in determining the ordinary peace *surplus,* which is my

tion. But I have not included all the sums there enumerated; nor have I admitted the Army savings in 1772, and some other smaller sums.

(b) This surplus, being the medium for the whole 12 years of peace, is less than that in p. 160, which is the medium at the end of this period, when the Sinking-Fund produced above a quarter more than it did at the beginning of it.

object, it was proper to exclude it, and to terminate the account at the commencement of the war.— I will only add, that Lord STAIR has also included more in the extraordinary receipts than I have; and, particularly, 700,000 l. which he suppofes the public gained by the TEA INDEMNITY.—— But this was only a compenfation made by the *Eaft-India* Company for the lofs which the public fuftained by taking off, in 1766, a part (or 1 s. *per* pound) of the duty on tea. In 1772 it was reftored; and the excife upon tea has fince, if I am rightly informed, produced as much as ever. *Before* 1766, it produced annually 474,091 l. Immediately (*a*) after 1766, it produced 341,284 l.— But in 1775, it produced near half a million.

Sketch of an Account of the Money drawn from the Public by the Taxes, before the Year 1776.

CUSTOMS in ENGLAND, being the medium of the payments into the Exchequer, for 3 years ending in 1773 (*b*) — — — £. 2,528,275

Amount of the EXCISES in ENGLAND, including the malt tax,

being

(*a*) I have here taken the average of two years before and after 1766.

(*b*) The annual medium of the payments into the Exchequer from the CUSTOMS in ENGLAND, for the laft five years, has

been

		£.
being the medium of 3 years ending in 1773	— —	4.649,892
Land Tax at 3 s.	— —	1.300,000

been 2.521,769 l.—In 1774 the payment into the Exchequer was 2.547,717 l.—In 1775, it was 2.476,302 l.—The produce of the Customs, therefore, has been given rather too high.

The produce of the Excises in England has been higher, in 1772 and 1775, than in any two years before 1776; but the average of any three succeſſive years, or of all the five years since 1770, will not differ much from the sum I have given.— In 1754, or the year before the laſt war, the Customs produced only 1.558,254 l.——The Excises, exclusive of the Malt-tax, produced 2.819,702 l,——And the whole revenue, exclusive of the Malt-tax and Land-tax at 2 s. was 5.097,617 l. —In 1753 the whole revenue was 5.189,745 l. And the appropriation or annual charge upon it, (conſiſting of the Civil Liſt, 834,443 l. intereſt of the national debt, exclusive of navy debt, 2.628,087 l. expences of management, 43;691 l. 4½ *per cent*. from the Leeward Iſlands 27,378 l. annuity to the late Duke of Cumberland 25,000 l. firſt-fruits and tenths of the Clergy 13,597 l. &c. &c.) was 3.733,713 l. The Sinking-Fund, therefore, produced 1.456,000 l.; which, added to 1.500,000 l. (the neat produce, at that time, of Land at 2 s. and Malt-tax) made the unappropriated revenue 2.956,032 l.— The expence of the peace eſtabliſhment, conſiſting of 10,000 seamen, and 18,857 landmen, was, in 1753 and 1754, (including an allowance for the increaſe of the Navy-debt) 2.400,000 l. nearly; which left an annual surplus in the national income of 556,000 l. *without* lotteries, and land at 2 s. This surplus (with land at 3 s.) has of late scarcely exceeded 300,000 l.; and, therefore, has not been a THIRD of what it was in the laſt peace, and before the reduction of intereſt to 3 *per cent*. was compleated.

[168]

Land Tax at 1 s. in the pound —	£. 450,000
Salt Duties, being the medium of the years 1765 and 1766 —	218,739
Duties on Stamps, Cards, Dice, Advertifements, Bonds, Leafes, Indentures, News-papers, Almanacks, &c. — —	280,788
Duties on houfes and windows, being the medium of 3 years ending in 1771 — —	385,369
Poft Office, Seizures, Wine Licences, Hackney Coaches, Tenths of the Clergy, &c. — —	250,000
Excises in Scotland, being the medium of 3 years ending in 1773	95,229
Customs in Scotland, being the medium of 3 years ending in 1773 — — —	68,369
Annual profit from Lotteries —	150,000
Inland taxes in Scotland, coinage duties, cafual revenues, fuch as the duties on Gum-Senega, American revenue, &c. — —	150,000
Expence of collecting the Excises in England, being the average of the years 1767 and 1768, when their produce was 4.531,075 l. *per ann.* 6 *per cent.* of the grofs produce --	297,887
Expence of collecting the Excifes in Scotland, being the medium	

of

of the years 1772 and 1773, and the difference between the grofs and nett produce——31 *per cent.* of the grofs produce — £. 43,254

Expence of collecting the Customs in England, being the average of 1771 and 1772, bounties included, and 15 *per cent.* of the grofs produce, exclufive of drawbacks and over-entries — — 468,703

N. B. The bounties for 1771 were 202,840 l.—for 1772, 172,468 l. The charges of management for 1771, were 276,434 l.

For 1772, 285,764 l. or 10 *per cent.* nearly.

Intereft of loans on the land tax at 4 s. expences of collection, militia, &c. — — 250,000

Perquisites, &c. to Cuftom-houfe officers, &c. fuppofed — — 250,000

Expence of collecting the Salt-duties in England, 10$\frac{1}{2}$ *per cent.* — 27,000

Bounties on fifh exported — — 18,000

Expence of collecting the duties on Stamps, Cards, Advertifements, &c. 5$\frac{1}{4}$ *per cent.* — — 18,000

Total £. 11,900,505

It

It muſt be ſeen, that this account is imperfect and defective. It is, however, ſufficient to prove, that the whole money raiſed DIRECTLY by the taxes, (excluſive of tithes, county rates, and the taxes which ſupport the poor,) cannot be much leſs than TWELVE MILLIONS. The *Earl of Stair* has in his papers made it to be above 400,000 l. more, by including in his eſtimate ſeveral articles which I have omitted; particularly, the intereſt and management on the equivalent to *Scotland*, the Scotch crown Revenues, Dutchy of *Cornwall* and *Lancaſter* Fines, &c. He has alſo given an eſtimate of the fees and perquiſites of office of every kind, and reckoned them at half a million; whereas, I have only reckoned the perquiſites of office at the *Cuſtom-houſe*.

I ſhould be inexcuſable were I to quit this ſubject, without taking notice of the particular gratitude due from the public to *Lord Stair*, for publiſhing his papers; and for ſtepping forth at this time to draw attention, by the weight of his name and character, to calculations, which, as he juſtly ſays, " it be-
" comes every man of property among us to
" underſtand; to awaken the nation from the
" lethargy into which the mockery of paper
" wealth has plunged it; and to bear his teſtimony
" againſt the preſent unnatural war."

POST-

POSTSCRIPT.

THE following POSTSCRIPT has been published only in a few of the laſt Editions of the *Obſervations on Civil Liberty*. It has been often referred to in the preceding work; and, therefore, it is neceſſary to give it a place here.

ACCOUNT *of Public Debts diſcharged, Money borrowed, and Annual Intereſt ſaved from* 1763 *to* 1775.

Debts paid off ſince 1763.	Annuity decreaſed.
£.	£. s.
1765— 870,888 funded, bearing intereſt at 4 *per cent.*	34,835 10
1.500,000 unfunded, 4 *per cent.*	60,000 00
1766—0.870,888 funded, 4 *per cent.*	34,835 10
1.200,000 unfunded, 4 —	48,000 00
1767—2.616,777 funded, 4 —	104,671 0
1768—2.625,000 funded, 4 —	105,000 0
1771—1.500,000 funded, 3 *per cent.*	45,000 0
1772—1.500,000 funded, 3 *per cent.*	45,000 0
1773— 800,000 unfunded, 3 —	24,000 0
1774—1.000,000 funded, 3 —	30,000 0
1775—1.000,000 funded, 3 —	30,000 0
Total 15.483,553	Total 561,342 0

In 1764, there was paid off 650,000 l. navy-debt; but this I have not charged, becaufe fcarcely equal to that annual increafe of the navy-debt for 1764, 1765, and 1766, which forms a part of the ordinary peace eftablifhment. The fame is true of 300,000 l. navy-debt, paid in 1767; of 400,000 l. paid in 1769; of 100,200 l. paid in 1770; 200,000 l. in 1771; 215,883 l. in 1772; and 200,000 l. in 1774.

Account of money borrowed and debts contracted fince 1763.

		£.	Annual intereft increafed.
Borrowed and funded, at 3 per cent. - in	1765	1,500,000	45,000
in	1766	1,500,000	45,000
in	1767	1,500,000	45,000
in	1768	1,900,000	57,000
Unfunded in	1774	250,000	7,500
Civil lift debt in	1775 (a)	500,000	
	Total	7,150,000	199,500

(a) This article was omitted in the former editions of this *Poftfcript*; and its infertion here makes the diminution of the public debts, fince 1763, half a million lefs than the fum at which it is taken in p. 104 and 108.——It might have been proper alfo to add, the excefs of Navy debts *contracted* above the Navy debts *difcharged*, from 1763 to 1775; and had this been done, the furplus in p. 165, would have been reduced to 150,000l.

From

[173]

From 15.483,553*l.* the total of debts difcharged, fubftract 7.150,000*l.* the total of debts contracted; and the remainder, or 8.333,553*l.* will be the diminution of the public debts fince 1763. Alfo, from 561,342*l.* the total of the decreafe of the annual intereft, fubtract 199,500*l.* (the total of its increafe), and the remainder, or 361,842*l.* will be the intereft or annuity faved fince 1763.—To this muft be added 12,537*l. per ann.* faved by changing a capital of 1.253,700*l.* (part of 20.240,000*l.*) from an intereft of 4 to 3 *per cent.* purfuant to an act of the 10th of George III.; alfo the life-annuities that have fallen in; and 7,500*l. per ann.* gained by the falling (in 1771) of 1.500,000*l.* from an intereft of $3\frac{1}{2}$ to 3 *per cent.*; which will make a faving in the whole of near 400,000*l. per annum:* And it is to this faving, together with the increafe of luxury, that the increafe of the *Sinking-Fund* for the laft ten years has been owing.

To the debts difcharged the following additions muft be made.

In 1764 there was paid towards difcharging the extraordinary expences of the army, 987,434*l.*: In 1765, thefe expences amounted to 404,496*l.*: In 1766, to 479,088*l.*—Total 1.871,018*l.*—— This fum is at leaft a million higher than the extraordinary expences of the army for three years in a time of peace. This excefs, being derived from the preceding war, muft be reckoned a debt left by the war. And the same is true of 1.106,000*l*. applied, in 1764, 1765, and 1766, towards satisfying *German* demands.——There are likewise some smaller sums of the same kind; such as subsidies to *Hesse-Cassel*, *Brunswick*, &c. And they may be taken at 200,000*l*.——The total of all these sums is 2.306,240 *l*.; which, added to 8.333,553*l*. makes the whole diminution of the public debt since 1763, to be 10.639,793*l*.

Soon after the peace in 1763, an unfunded debt, amounting to 6.983,553*l*. was funded on the *Sinking Fund*, and on new duties on wine and cyder, at 4 *per cent*. There has been since borrowed and funded on coals exported, window-lights, &c. 6.400,000*l*. The funded debt, therefore, has increased since the war 13.383,553*l*. It has decreased (as appears from page 171) 11.983,553*l*.; and, consequently, there has been on the whole an addition to it of 1.400,000*l*.——During seven years, from 1767 to 1774, 1.415,883*l*. navy-debt was paid off. See page 172. But, as this is a debt arising from constant deficiencies in the peace estimates for the navy, it is a part of the current peace expences.—In 1768 this debt was (*a*) 1.226,915*l*.—In 1774 it was 1.850,000*l*.; and consequently, though 1 415,883*l*. was paid off, an addition was made to it, in seven years, of 623,085*l*. It increased, therefore, at the rate of 291,000*l*. *per ann*.

(*a*) See *The Present State of the Nation*, page 26.

THE

THE paper from which I have taken the following account, came into my hands after almost the whole of this work had been printed off. It contains a fact of so much importance, that I cannot satisfy myself without laying it before the public. ——— In a Committee of Congress in *June* 1775, a declaration was drawn up containing an offer to Great Britain, " that
" the Colonies would not only continue to grant
" extraordinary aids in time of war, but also, if
" allowed a free commerce, pay into the Sink-
" ing-Fund such a sum annually for one hun-
" dred years, as should be *more* than sufficient
" in that time, if faithfully applied, to extinguish
" all the present debts of Britain. Or, provided
" this was not accepted, that, to remove the
" groundless jealousy of *Britain* that the Colonies
" aimed at Independence and an abolition of the
" Navigation Act, which, in truth, they had never
" intended; and also, to avoid all future disputes
" about the right of making that and other Acts
" for regulating their commerce for the general
" benefit, they would enter into a covenant with
" *Britain*, that she should fully possess and exercise
" that right for *one hundred years* to come."

At the end of the *Observations on Civil Liberty*, I had the honor of laying before the public the Earl of *Shelburne*'s plan of Pacification with the Colonies.

Colonies. In that plan, it is particularly proposed, that the Colonies should grant an annual supply to be carried to the Sinking Fund, and unalienably appropriated to the discharge of the public debt.—It must give this excellent Peer great pleasure to learn, from this resolution, that even this part of his plan, as well as all the other parts, would, most probably, have been accepted by the Colonies. For though the resolution only offers the alternative of either a *free* trade, with extraordinary aids and an annual supply, or an *exclusive* trade confirmed and extended; yet there can be little reason to doubt, but that to avoid the calamities of the present contest, BOTH would have been consented to; particularly, if, on our part, such a revisal of the laws of trade had been offered as was proposed in Lord Shelburne's plan.

The preceding resolution was, I have said, drawn up in a Committee of the Congress. But it was not entered in their minutes; a severe Act of Parliament happening to arrive at that time, which determined them not to give the sum proposed in it.

F I N I S.

www.ingramcontent.com/pod-product-compliance
Lightning Source LLC
Chambersburg PA
CBHW020239170426
43202CB00008B/139